1st - 10ª

Agrarian Kentucky

THOMAS D. CLARK

THE UNIVERSITY PRESS OF KENTUCKY

Illustrations by William B. Crouch

Research for The Kentucky Bicentennial Bookshelf
is assisted by a grant from the
National Endowment for the Humanities.
Views expressed in the Bookshelf do not
necessarily represent those of the Endowment.

ISBN: 0-8131-0237-5

Library of Congress Catalog Card Number: 77-73703

A statewide cooperative scholarly publishing agency
serving Berea College, Centre College of Kentucky,
Eastern Kentucky University, The Filson Club,
Georgetown College, Kentucky Historical Society,
Kentucky State University, Morehead State University,
Murray State University, Northern Kentucky University,
Transylvania University, University of Kentucky,
University of Louisville, and Western Kentucky University.

Editorial and Sales Offices: Lexington, Kentucky 40506

Contents

Preface

Kentuckians have stamped upon their schools, churches, court days, county fairs—on every phase of their lives—the deep impress of the land. It is relatively simple to confirm this fact at any period in the commonwealth's history. Most revealing are educational statistics which reflect the distinctly rural cast of mind. If the rural Kentuckian during the past two centuries had invested his material resources as recklessly as he supported his public schools he would have been more thoroughly bankrupted than the biblical prodigal son. For almost a century and a half the people elected representatives who set too low educational standards for their offspring, and the commonwealth still has not been able to overcome the effects of this cultural denial.

By contrast over the centuries country churches have been common gathering places where rural people have filled both spiritual and social voids, and where they have sounded the depths of their personal commitments. The history of institutional religion in Kentucky is thoroughly and intimately interwoven with that of secular life. From the era of the great revivals in the early 1800s to the most recent emotional outpourings of snake-handling pentecostal meetings, Kentucky country churches with simplistic approaches to life have conditioned rural responses to public issues.

For over a century broad areas of Kentucky remained completely isolated, socially and economically. Not until the dawning of an industrial age during the first decades of this century, were breaches made in the barriers which held hundreds of thousands of Kentuckians cultural captives of the land they cherished. Actually it took the tradition-shattering national depression of the 1930s to break through the bindings of social and economic peonage in some parts of the state.

The irony and the tragedy of Kentucky history have been the persistence of centuries-old inequities. Under sectional demarcations have prevailed astonishing inequalities in all areas of life in the commonwealth. The very terms politicians have used over the years to designate Kentucky political reactions have reflected qualitative differences in the conditions of human existence. It would be hard to imagine greater contrasts than those which existed in the 1880s between rowdy hill country raftsmen and anglophile scions of rich Bluegrass estates or, in more basic economic terms, those between a highly developed central Kentucky stock farm and the minimal homesteads of Mountain and Purchase subsistence farms.

Too much of the Kentucky population never experienced sustained prosperity. Far too many of the people were and still are held in a state of chronic social and economic "arrest" to permit consideration of more than the most elementary human needs. Definitive sectional divisions with pronounced cultural differences have prevented Kentuckians from uniting in sustained support of solutions to state problems.

Historically, Kentuckians have felt comfortable and cooperative with each other only in four shared ideas or experiences. The first has been common love of land, no matter how much its appearance or productivity varied. Second, from the outset Kentuckians have nurtured a nostalgia which has prompted them to appeal to the past without troubling to determine its factual foundations. Third, from the moment conflict began to develop between Virginia settlers and the overlords at Boonesboro, a stream of "managed" politics has flowed out from the tiny rivulets of the magisterial districts, through a constantly expanding number of courthouses and rings to Frankfort. Finally, with the commonwealth's economy based almost solely upon the land, there has prevailed an opposition to taxation, no matter what constructive common purpose it might support.

These are only some of the basic facts. Overall life in rural Kentucky has been colored with moments of simple joys, deep sorrows, and generous streaks of self-generated humor. For most Kentuckians their history is translated into the personal terms of revered ancestors, political and military heroes, self-sacrificing pioneers, unforgivable family enemies, and uninhibited scoundrels who have furnished them moments of vicarious enjoyment. In retrospect the way of the countryside seemed the good way of life. It was one which drew stout nourishment from plain honesty and human effort. It was a way of life in which humans responded to other humans with lavish help and unstinting hospitality.

The folk past of Kentucky has been a rich source for press and book copy. From the outset editors and reporters recognized they could strike responsive emotional chords with stories of rural life and character. In more modern decades columnists for both folksy country weeklies and sophisticated metropolitan dailies have endeared themselves to Kentuckians with warmly reminiscent stories and broad pen strokes of rural humor. Somewhere it did matter to somebody why a hound dog whirled round-and-round in preparation to lie down or why a tumblebug worked so hard to mold his ball of cow dung. It mattered to be reminded of ground hog days, the efficacy of buckeyes, and the virtues of Barlow knives. Agrarianism has provided both savor and substance in the writings of Kentucky authors. Almost unanimously novelists have cast their writings against a boldly etched backdrop of land and rural life. From James Lane Allen to Wendell Berry they have found on the land backgrounds and characters for stories of social, economic, and intellectual struggles.

In their own narrow translation of the puritan ethic, Kentuckians have viewed farming as the seminal way of life. From furrow and countryside have sprung pure and just, if not noble, citizens. They have been the natural legatees of democracy, and the mainstays of the Republic. They have fallen under the shadow of the politicians' faithless gestures to "the people," and they have been victimized by broken promises and deceptions. Nevertheless only a reckless politician would suggest support of measures injurious to the Kentucky agrarian way of life. For generations of Kentucky office seekers the farmer and his plights have been good issueless shields. His causes could be proclaimed on the hustings in loud calls for reform and later noiselessly shunted underneath the vortex of legislative maneuverings. It has ever been so.

The rolling country hills and valleys of Kentucky present a massive and alluring canvas. Dotted with peaceful farmsteads and modest cabins, the land collectively represents the substance and spirit of home. Its rurality has been the womb of a nostalgic history into which Kentuckians have often retreated. It has furnished the substance by which the people have conditioned their minds, forged their reactions to public issues, waged their battles with nature; and to which finally they have surrendered their bodies. Through the land they have bound themselves to a region and a way of life and have asserted a fierce provincial pride which gives spiritual essence to the commonwealth itself.

1

THE LAND, ITS PROMISE
AND ITS PATTERN

The EASTERN KENTUCKY woods bordering on the Rockcastle River were greening in mid-March 1775, when Daniel Boone and his trailblazing companions hacked their way through the massive tangle of "dead brush" along that stream. At the western edge of the deadening they burrowed their way through a vast canebrake which all but obscured the land from view. Crossing the narrow saddle gap which separated the hills of the Roundstone country from the Bluegrass savannah land, this advance party of the Transylvania Company was ready to set foot in the fertile promised land. The youthful North Carolinian, Felix Walker, grew poetic when the welcome scene opened before his eyes. He recorded in his brief travel journal, "and as the cane ceased, we began to discover the plains of Kentucky. A new sky and strange earth seemed to be presented to our view. So rich a soil we had never seen before; covered with clover in full bloom, the woods were abounding with wild game—turkeys so numerous that it might be said they appeared as one flock, universally scattered in the woods. It appeared that nature, in the profusion of her bounty, had spread a feast for all that lives, both for the animal and rational world. A sight so delightful to our feelings and grateful to our feelings, almost inclined in imitation of Columbus, in transport to kiss the soil of Kentucky, as he hailed and saluted the sand on his first setting foot in the shores of America."

Standing atop the westernmost face of the Kentucky Knobs, Walker and his companions no doubt felt they had just arrived at the fields of Elysium. Behind the exuberant author and his companions lay the great virgin forest of eastern Kentucky. Before them lay the undulating plateau of the Bluegrass. Other eyes, those of Indian and long hunter, had gazed across this same vista, and in the immediate future hundreds of anxious immigrants would enter this land. These immigrants plodded westward over muddy and steep mountain paths, forded angry streams, and kept eyes peeled for Indian attackers. They came as settlers to establish yeoman family homesteads or as speculators seeking to locate and claim large tracts of land.

Geologists have since been more precise than dazzled settlers were in their descriptions of the region's geological ages, soil analysis, forest cover, streams, and mineral deposits. For the long hunters and land scouts the land broke down into the simplest terms of woods, canebrakes, river bottoms, mountain walls, rich soils, prospective pastures, and cabin sites. Bounding on the east were the Appalachian highlands which at eye level were composed of steep ridges, narrow river and creek bottoms, forbidding coves and glades, and rubble-strewn mountain shoulders and stream beds. All of these promised an existence of social isolation and neglect. The sheltering stand of towering deciduous timber had ages ago masked the hills beneath a cover of green. This timber forced the settler-farmer to expend prodigious energy to clear open spaces. Though the central plain also was forest covered, the land's evenness reduced the burden of hacking fields and pastures out of the timber. Thus geography determined the nature of the society and economy which would come to exist in all of Kentucky, particularly in the Bluegrass.

Sharp variations in the lay and nature of the lands divided the social and economic structure of the future state into three or four distinctive sections. The fertile, limestone-based Bluegrass lands were destined to sustain a prosperous agrarian economy and a way of life comparable to that of rural England or Tidewater Virginia. By contrast the Appalachian highlands drew immigrants into river valleys, pinched coves, and even onto hilltop plateaus, and bound them to a subsistence type of agriculture and an arrested mode of social life. Farming land was at a premium even for the first settlers and became more so as the population expanded.

Graphically a social-minded Kentucky geologist, A. M. Miller, wrote of the Knob country civilization as late as 1919: "The inhabitants (of the Knobs) are for the most part proverbially poor, getting only a scanty subsistence from the soil, supplemented by what they obtain from marketing tanbark (generally the bark of the chestnut oak) and a few railroad ties. A number of ax handle, pick handle and stave mills, established by outside enterprise, work up the oak and hickory which can still be found suitable for such milling purposes." The people of this peripheral area related to the mountains behind them rather than to Bluegrass society to the west and north. Miller believed the people were quite willing to accept and perpetuate marginal social and economic conditions. Farming methods, domestic economy, and political outlook were all shaped by the quality and nature of the soil. Even "In food preparation this region should be classed with the mountains. One meets here with the same large soda biscuits, yellow from excess soda, with the inevitable eggs which swam in grease as they fried, with scrambled pie, with sorghum, and with what by every country store in both regions is sold for coffee, but which bears little resemblance in taste." Such was the historical mark of the land which could be identified in human relationships, methods of cultivation, implements, and buildings. Elsewhere the patterns of society and agriculture were to be repeated. Along the Green, the Barren, and the Cumberland rivers and the short bight of the Tennessee River in the sprawling hinterlands the rural pattern of life was implanted.

As in the eastern and northern regions southwestern Kentucky lands varied in quality from rock-and-clay-poor to bottomless loams enriching their owners year after year.

East of the mountains after 1774 there built up a land hysteria which sometimes had little relationship to the realities of the Kentucky region to the West. Praise of the "garden" was extravagant. Gen. Levi Todd described the central countryside as "delightful beyond conception" and productive of lush growths of weeds, wild grasses, and cane—a fertility which would be equally productive of field crops. Even that seasoned land scout George Rogers Clark wrote in 1775, three months after he had arrived in Kentucky, "A richer and more beautiful country than this I believe has never been seen in America yet." Word of mouth descriptions, the bustle of emigrants packing up to leave for the western waters, the excitement of the departure of the traveling church groups, the propaganda of the land speculators—all of these noised the news of Kentucky's promises abroad.

Agents for the "garden" described it in extravagant terms. Fortescue Cuming told his readers "Perhaps there is not on the earth a naturally richer country than the area of sixteen hundred square miles of which Lexington is the center. . . ." John Campbell viewed the Falls of the Ohio and its flood plain. The rising village of Louisville he regarded as nature's temporary magazine or depository to receive the products of an extensive land, where "the Fertility of the Soil, and Facility of Cultivation . . . fit it for producing Commodities of great Value with little Labour; the Wholesomeness of the Waters, and Serenity of the Air . . . render it healthy; and the Property may be so easily acquired, we may, with Certainty, affirm that it will in a short time be equalled by few Places on the American Continent." Every traveler and scheming promoter sang the praise of a country offering lands for as little as twelve to fifteen shillings an acre.

Almost countless descriptions of the land of Kentucky appeared in immigrants' letters, travelers' accounts, and newspapers. Occasionally in the late nineteenth century a pioneer boasted of the promise of the land. About him grew towering trees, matted canebrakes, and giant weeds to support his judgment. Nowhere else on the globe was there a greater variety of first-quality virgin timber than inside that great fold of land between the Pine Mountain range and the Ohio and Mississippi rivers. There were tulip poplars, chestnuts, black and white walnuts, more than a dozen types of oaks, beeches, hop hornbeam, cottonwoods, three varieties of pines, hemlock, black and sweet gums, black cherry, buckeye, mulberry, two kinds of locusts, and four varieties of maples.

Possibly the greatest irony of Kentucky history is the fact that the land was originally settled by an agrarian-pastoral people who had so little immediate regard for the forest as a basic but exhaustible resource. As the pioneers were ignorant of the science of silviculture and land-forest management, they passed on a legacy of mismanagement to future generations. Moreover, mountain and knob forests exercised a powerful isolative and deterrent influence on founding an agrarian society.

Early Kentuckians classified their lands in three generalized categories, which also describe degrees of productivity. The soils of the central area and those of the alluvial basins were considered to be of the first quality. Second-rate lands rested upon a thinner soil base and were less productive. Those in the third-rate category were the steep ridges and "hot" and dry mountain and knob plateaus. The last two classifications covered a large portion of the state. John Filson, land salesman and pioneer Kentucky historian, wrote that the countryside "in some places, is nearly level; in others not so much so; in others again hilly, but moderately, and in some places there is most water. The levels are . . . interspersed with small risings, and declivities, which form a beautiful prospect. A great deal of the soil is amazingly fertile; some not so good, and some poor. The inhabitants distinguish its quality by first, second, and third rate lands; and scarcely any such thing as a marsh or swamp is to be found." The soils of Kentucky differ from most of those beyond the Ohio. Except for the rich alluvial shoulders which taper down to the streams, the friable soils of Kentucky derive from constantly decaying underlying rocks and are of "immediate derivation," as distinguished from those transported by water and glaciers. In 1876, Nathaniel Southgate Shaler wrote, "Beginning with the lowest rocks, the soils of the Blue or Cambrian Limestone are those of first quality, and are surpassed by no soils in any country for fertility and endurance."

It is little wonder that the population rose from zero in 1774 to more than 220,000 in 1800. Harry Toulmin, liberal Englishman and college president, said that the earliest immigrants to reach Kentucky in the final quarter of the eighteenth century were husbandmen who sought land on which to locate homesteads and to begin the business of farming. The process was indeed simple. If a farmer fetched over the mountains a few basic tools he was "In such a situation (after building his house which cost him little more than his labor) he should produce some dung hill fowls, a cow and a breeding sow. The fowls will produce eggs for his family, the cow milk and butter, if she is taken care of; and the sow will produce two, if not three, litters of pigs within the year." Thus Toulmin drew the blueprint for Kentucky's subsistence mode of farming.

The early settlement of Kentucky introduced to American frontier history two infernal institutions which persisted with the tenacity of jimsonweeds and sassafras sprouts. One was the squatters who moved on to lands of their choice without attending to the niceties of legal confirmation or respect for prior ownership. The other was the establishment of the right of preemption (or prior claim) which came to be used as an instrument of claim and as an emotional and political hold on the land.

The population movement to the west gained greater momentum after the end of the French and Indian War than did the spread of orderly political authority. Whether the famous Proclamation of 1763, prohibiting settlement west of the Alleghenies, was largely responsible for this state of affairs is debatable. Technically, if not actually, Virginia was bound by both the proclamation and subsequent geographically restrictive Indian treaties, especially those of Hard Labor and Fort Stanwix in 1768. In less than a decade the caveats of both the proclamation and the treaties were largely ignored or forgotten. The great rash of land prospecting and surveying in the Ohio Valley in 1774–75 led to feverish interest in Kentucky. It also established the ensnarlment of the Kentucky land system for all time to come. Virginia could not make an orderly survey of the Kentucky country before settlers were admitted to the region. In fact, none of the early private surveys had official sanction or standing. To have surveyed the region of Kentucky in the years of the Revolutionary War would have been too costly, and there were no technically qualified persons to undertake such a task. In any event Indians on both sides were too resistant to have permitted such a survey, and in Richmond political interests were focused elsewhere.

By 1776 Kentucky's land system, if it could be called such, was hopelessly mired in overlapping and dual claims, squatter rivalries, unregistered deeds, and vague boundaries. When the General Assembly undertook to bring order to this chaotic mess in the midst of war, it was too late. Enacted that year was the first of several land laws which undertook to prescribe the terms by which a homesteader could lay sustainable claim to a farm. With democratic idealism ascendant, Thomas Jefferson looked upon the public lands of the West as a bed in which to "seed democracy." He envisioned a band of happy cottagers living the rural good life and drawing their livelihood from diligently tended farmsteads. The law of 1776 contained the fairly dramatic clause "That no family shall be entitled to the allowance granted to settlers by this act, *Unless they have made a crop of corn in that country, or resided there at least one year since the time of their settlement.*" Then the politically conscious legislators all but invalidated their law by providing for preemption rights for squatters.

Back of the passage and attempt to administer the land law of 1776 were some interesting facts. First, the land companies, claiming almost boundless tracts, found themselves defenseless against tenacious settlers. Second, the settlers came on the American scene in sufficient numbers to generate a significant amount of political influence to protect their interests. Third, the original provision for the granting of 400 acres to an individual claimant reflected the belief of both legislators and western pioneers that this was the amount of

7

land a single yeoman family could in time bring under cultivation and pasturage. Subsequent petitions of settlers and military veterans reflected strong feelings about the land question. It was indeed significant that in the formative years of settling Kentucky veterans of the Revolutionary and Indian wars were prominent in debating it. In addition, lobbying activities of land companies and rising western squires forced further consideration of the public land issue in the most pinching times of the Revolution. In June 1779, under the sponsorship of George Mason, the General Assembly enacted a second land law which, among other provisions, validated the Virginia-controlled Loyal Land Company's claim to 200,000 acres in Kentucky. Under the new law a settler actually on the land before January 1, 1778, was granted right to 400 acres upon the payment of a nominal fee and could preempt 1,000 acres more on the most generous terms. The law also established what turned out to be the infamous land office in Kentucky.

Instead of "seeding democracy" as anticipated, the law of 1779 opened the way for speculators to plaster Kentucky with vast claims. It was now possible for a shrewd manipulator to gather in original and preemption claims almost at will. In time Kentucky settlers filled the records of the Virginia government with petitions protesting abuses or trying to establish valid claims. Later petitioners turned to the Kentucky counties for relief.

The land laws of 1776 and 1779 created the suspicion that Kentucky titles granted by Virginia would be invalidated either because of imperfect and improper registration or because prior claimants could establish better title. In 1780, a year of furious immigrant activity in Kentucky, Thomas Paine, the famous revolutionary pamphleteer, turned his biting fury on Virginia and its western land claims. In his pamphlet *Public Good*, Paine actually argued the cause of the small landless states faced with mountainous debts and impetuous veterans' claims for bounties expected for service in the Revolutionary War. This publication's garbled contents got abroad by word of mouth. An impression was created in Kentucky that land titles resting upon the authority of Virginia might be invalidated. Kentucky petitioners who communicated their troubles and worries to Richmond reflected the anxiety created by news of Paine's writings. At the same time two scoundrels named Galloway and Pomeroy appeared in Lexington and Louisville spreading rumors that no prior climant had valid deeds. So unsettling was this propaganda that the pair was dealt with summarily and run out of Kentucky. Nevertheless the Paine, Galloway, and Pomeroy incidents reflected public sensitivity over the issues of sanctity of deeds and dependability of land boundaries. Few issues have stirred the emotions of so many Kentuckians since 1776.

In 1802 Francois A. Michaux, the observant French botanist, wrote that the enthusiastic inrush of immigrants to Kentucky in the last quarter of the eighteenth century sometimes reached 20,000 persons per year. Prices for desirable lands in the more choice locations soared. Rogues profited from the land trade and the trickery associated with it. Promoters were known to have prepared maps showing false rivers and towns in order to ensnare unwary investors. Michaux thought "This rapid increase might have been much greater but for one particular circumstance, which prevents immigration to those districts; I allude to the difficulty of establishing claims to landed property; for all of the states of the Union, it is in this Kentucky that such claims are most the subject of controversy. I never stopped at a house of a single inhabitant, who did not appear convinced of the validity of his own title, while he doubted that of his neighbor." The Frenchman attributed this condition to the ignorance of surveyors, the difficulties of much of the terrain, the early Indian menace, and the constant changing of land boundaries. "In short," he wrote, "there are lots of a thousand acres, in which every hundred is the subject of contest." This was, of course, a surface view of the situation.

Nearer to the land itself was the fact that settlers streamed into Kentucky from western Pennsylvania, the Carolinas, Maryland, and Virginia, and most of them brought Virginia land office and treasury warrants. They came expecting that they could locate land and settle down to the good life of pioneering. They quickly discovered that Virginia military warrants and preemption rights exercised under the terms of the law of 1779 took precedence over all other certificates. This circumstance caused further confusion and unrest, and every month competition for good lands in the central area grew more intense. Litigation became furious and land prices advanced phenomenally. On the heels of settlers came lawyers to defend or to disavow shaky claims or to prosecute pesky squatters. Names such as Breckinridge, Wallace, Muter, Innis, McDowell, and Clay were early associated with both the Kentucky bar and the beleaguered land system.

A historical plat of landholdings for almost any township-sized area in Kentucky, outside of the Jackson Purchase, would reveal an unbelievably snarled maze of overlapping boundaries. Aside from shortages of competent surveyors and money, Kentucky presented physiographical obstacles to the creation of an orderly grid of land patterns. In 1775 almost 90 percent of the present state's surface was covered with heavy virgin timber which would make the establishment of magnetic lines laborious and costly, even if the surface had been as smooth and level as a floor. But almost three-fifths of that surface is either mountainous or rough hilly terrain, which has always complicated the task of correct mathematical computations. Consequently, much of the job of scientific surveying was left undone. Application of the vague system called metes and bounds could scarcely be validated through precise survey.

The surface pattern of Kentucky reflects the entanglement of land claims and the scars of litigation, almost as eloquently as do the bulging files of lawsuits brought under the original laws of land grants, the ignorance of surveyors, and the records of land hunger of original settlers. Like a quilt created in a frontier quilting party, the land plots of Kentucky lie about in side patches, darts, wavering lines, and wayward fence rows. A common factor in most original Kentucky landholds is revealed in the monotonous testimonials of warranty deed descriptions declaring that original owners planted patches of corn, raised pole cabins, declared claims for 400 acres, and preempted 1,000 more. This declaration was repeated thousands of times in the nineteenth century in an attempt to sustain the sanctity of "warranty deeds."

The physical and legalistic background of the Kentucky land is a story of excitement, of tragedy, and sometimes of humor. It was, however, the bigger pattern of human associations which had fundamental historical meaning. For Kentuckians, whether prosperous Bluegrass farmers with pastures dotted with good grade livestock, with thousands of hempen shocks, hogsheads of tobacco, and smokehouses crammed with cured meats, or mountain yeomen clinging to slanted ridges growing small patches of subsistence grain, living in log cabins with facades adorned with strings of shucky beans, dried fruits, and herbs, the land was a source of refuge and a way of life. It shaped the history of the state, flavored the culture and the politics, infused the Kentucky personality, and prospered or impoverished people with a decisive hand. Beyond the mere material facts associated with the exploitation of the land, it was earth translated into terms of affection and motherhood that held in nostalgic grip, first the immigrant settler, and then the "native." There was more than whimsical truth in the sentimental observation of a land auctioneer that, "I am offering you in this sale the very nipple of the bosom of mother Kentucky."

By 1787 Kentucky lands drew settlers like a mighty magnet draws filings. Jedediah Morse said in his *American Geography*, "The rapid population of the western country has not only astonished America itself, but must amaze Europe, when they enter into the views and increase of this growing empire." He said Kentucky contained 100,000 souls in 1792. "I have known," he wrote, "upwards of 10,000 immigrants to arrive in the state of Kentucky within one year, and from 4 to 10,000 in several other years." A more authoritative counting of heads indicated there were 73,677 in 1790, 220,955 in 1800, and more than a half million in 1830. Immigrants came from "home" to establish new farms and a fresh way of agrarian life. In a phenomenally short time their annual harvests added to the mounting cargoes shipped by flatboats into the precarious

Spanish-controlled market. Back of rising population and farm production was the human story of the creation of a way of rural life which was repeated thousands of times.

Mary Coburn Dewees was a literate young Pennsylvania matron who traveled the grueling overland and river route from Philadelphia to Lexington with her family in the winter of 1787–88. On a cold 29 January 1788, Mary Dewees arrived "home," and in a paean of joyfulness she concluded her journal, "I have this day reached South Elkhorn and am much pleased with it." She wrote, "Tis a snug little cabin about nine miles from Lexington on a pretty ascent surrounded by sugar trees, a beautiful pond a little distance from the house, with an excellent spring not far from the door. I can assure you I have enjoyed more happiness the few days I have been here than I have experienced these four or five years past. I have my little family together and am full of expectation of seeing better days." In the immigrant streams annually arriving in Kentucky there came hundreds of "Marys" full of thankfulness that they could settle their families atop pleasant knolls shaded by sugar trees.

A more capacious dreamer than Mary Dewees was the exuberant British agriculturalist Arthur Young, who told prospective English immigrants Kentucky's climate was warmer in winter and cooler in summer than that of the British Isles. "The climate of England, next to taxation (a term including all public payments, whatever the object, or whoever the receiver), is the worst circumstance belonging to it," said Young. He advised Englishmen to improve their lots in both instances by moving to the new country. For five or six thousand pounds sterling, a family could plant itself on 5,000 solid acres of central Kentucky land, or five families could colonize 25,000 acres and live "in the midst of boundless plenty, and be carried through the two first years: let any person compare the situation of such a family; and the same living on 200£, or 300£, a year in England, paying, as men do pay in England, to king, church, and poor. If five families thus fixed on a contiguous 25,000 acres, they would have everything in America they could wish for in any country. . . ." Arthur Young failed to mention the fact that Americans also paid taxes, often reluctantly.

The packets of precious garden and field seeds settlers had lugged overland produced encouraging crops by the second year of settlement, and the new grounds were fallowed and ready for full production. Papers of tobacco seeds had grown into fields of ripening weed by the early 1780s, and there was pressing need for a market. The same was true of corn, rye, fruits, and cured meats. Ensnarled in a diplomatic tangle was the question of free access to the western river system. In 1785 westerners had angrily protested the proposed Jay Treaty, which would have closed to them the central river gate for a quarter of a century—long enough to have strangled the frontier with its own produce. There rapidly emerged strong political sentiment for national assurances that navigational channels would be kept open and free. At the foot of the Mississippi, however, there was confusion. Spain's possession of West Florida and control especially of the vital entrepôt of the Isle of Orleans made free passage of American boats and goods through that market almost fortuitous.

In June 1787 the scheming trader-politician James Wilkinson embarked from the Kentucky River landing before present-day Frankfort with a flotilla of boats loaded with tobacco and other agricultural products. Earlier, some of the famous long hunters had shipped caches of furs and skins by canoe to the downriver French market. Wilkinson's trading venture, however, was more important. The wily general was masterful at combining political intrigue with sharp commercial dealings. At Natchez he outtalked the Spanish intendant and drifted on to New Orleans and the center of Spain's North American authority. If the persuasive emissary could provide assurances of actions favoring Spain by Kentuckians, who then were seriously debating territorial separation from Virginia, he could gain for himself most favorable trade advantages. Such assurances depended, however, upon his ability to convince his fellow separation convention delegates back in Danville to approve Spain's retention of its strategic position in the Mississippi Valley. The realistic purpose of this intrigue was to open the western rivers to Kentucky farmers and, for Wilkinson personally, to gain a corner on the tobacco market as he earlier had attempted to do with the state's salt trade. Wilkinson had a yearning for riches, and for the power and prestige that money brought. There was a sharp difference between the $2.50 per hundred weight paid along the Kentucky for tobacco and the $9.50 which it brought on the New Orleans market. Plenty of tobacco was being grown on newly opened Kentucky farms, and the cost of drifting it aboard flatboats to the more remunerative market was modest. The opening of the Mississippi trade by James Wilkinson involved Kentucky farmers in intrigue, diplomatic maneuvers, and political pressures for the next two decades.

Kentuckians in 1794 had their edenic dream shattered by Alexander Hamilton's federal tax gatherers. The United States excise levy was magnified into oppressive proportions by Kentucky farmer-distillers, just as it had been in western Pennsylvania. At a called meeting in Lexington in 1793 irate farmers protested to state legislators and congressmen that payment of the whiskey tax in specie was impossible, especially since there was such grave uncertainty about the free use of the Mississippi River. The farmers offered to pay the collector of internal revenue in farm produce and let him haul it to market to collect his money. Thomas Marshall, collector of internal revenue for the Kentucky District, was as unpopular as Colonel John Neville in western Pennsylvania. The direct action of President Washington and the use of state militia forces chilled the defiant threats of Kentuckians to resist tax payments, but not their zeal to make whiskey. Bountiful crops of corn, rye, and fruits were converted into whiskey and brandy to be shipped aboard flatboats to the New Orleans market.

Other farmstead industries early began the processing of commodities for sale to the outside market. Families gathered large quantities of hardwood ashes and pork scraps to convert into soap for the river trade. In time many a flatboat manifest listed the gelatinous alkaline substance as a substantial item in its cargo. Along with barrels of lye soap went tubs of butter. Everywhere in the central region of the state there sprang up rope walks. In midsummer 1790 John Hamilton had begun making rope at Francis Dill's farm two miles south of Lexington. Five years later the famous mercantile firm of Thomas Hart and Son advertised in the *Kentucky Gazette* that they had begun the manufacture of rope from native hemp, and they solicited farmers to bring in fibers. Primitive devices for twisting cordage creaked through the years at numerous stands creating untold yards of rope, much of which was supplied to the western boat trade. As the cotton industry expanded in the developing Old Southwest much of the hemp crop was woven into bagging with which to wrap ginned bales.

The most common processing industry was the water mills which ground corn and small grains into meal and flour. By 1802 flour had become the most important processed Kentucky agricultural commodity sold on the western market. The boast was that Kentucky wheat made unusually good bread, and by the turn of the nineteenth century there was scarcely a free-flowing stream along the Kentucky River in the Bluegrass that was not dammed by one or more grain mills. Many of the great burrs of these mills were chiseled from local rock ledges; heavy wooden beams were hewn from nearby woods and fitted into sturdy mill houses to withstand the constant pounding of the whirling stones. In time, hundreds of thousands of barrels of grist were shipped down the Mississippi to be marketed and to be consumed as far away as western Europe.

By the turn of the nineteenth century the rapidly expanding commodities trade returned almost $2.25 million. This trade early established Kentuckians as restless and aggressive participants in western politics and economics. While farmers, housewives, distillers, and cordwainers produced growing mounds of commodities, untrained boatwrights labored about creek mouths fitting and mauling green timbers into tightly caulked cargo boxes to transport these farm products downstream. The lumbering western river "arks" were made of heavy, sawn timber pegged together with wooden pins and gaping seams rammed tight with hempen oakum. These boats ranged in length from thirty to ninety feet and in width from fifteen to thirty feet. Some were fitted with tight cargo holds, while others were only partially sheltered. These clumsy vessels were manned by from four to twenty men who handled stern, side, and bow sweeps. Driven by river currents, the boats were both awkward to handle and exceedingly vulnerable to accidents and costly disasters. A single snag or a merciless eddy could destroy everything. Drifting out of tiny lateral streams, farmers turned boatmen took with them the fruits of a year's labor and the hopes of future prosperity on the land. More than this, the Kentucky boatmen collectively comprised a tremendous western political force which demanded both national and international accommodation.

Within five years after Wilkinson's profitable and controversial voyage rugged backwoodsmen were steering sluggish crafts past perilous sucks and draws of the Ohio and Mississippi rivers to reach New Orleans. There they met ship captains from Britain, France, New England, and the West Indies. The Kentucky boats were laded with corn in the shuck and in barrels, tobacco packed in 1200 pound hogsheads, whiskey, brandy, and cider royal, hempen rope and bagging, salt pork, tubs of lard, piggins of butter, hides, barrels of soap, and tons of flour. Each passing year the country boats grew larger and more elaborate. And their crews seemed to become rowdier. In their loud proclamations of nationalism and free rights of access to land and river they raised fears in Spanish officials and stirred major diplomatic questions between the United States and Spain. Upstream Kentuckians had orated since 1787 on the subject of freeing the Mississippi for full access to boatmen-farmers. Drafters of resolutions were sure to include a plea on the subject. A sample was the resolve in November 1786 by the delegates to the Separation Convention in Danville, "That the common right of navigating the Mississippi, and of communicating with other nations through this channel, be considered as the bountiful gift of nature to the United States, as proprietors of the territories watered by the said river and its eastern branches."

The French agents who visited Kentucky in the fall of 1793 assured the people, "From government you have nothing even to hope. They never did intend—nor will they ever invest you with the right to use the Mississippi. Its procurement depends solely on ourselves. And this, my fellow citizens, is the *crisis*—the critical moment." It was indeed a crisis, as Kentuckians were ready to take up arms against Spain. The agent Lachaise told the Democratic Society in Lexington on 14 May 1794, "That causes unforeseen [George Washington and Thomas Jefferson] had put a stop to the march of two thousand brave Kentuckians, who were about to go and put an end to the Spanish despotism on the Mississippi; where Frenchmen and Kentuckians, united under the banners of France, might have made one nation, the happiest in the world; so perfect was their sympathy." The Washington administration did not view direct action by Kentucky farmers in so rosy a light. Nevertheless, the importance of the Mississippi River to Kentuckians was drilled into politicians by resolutions, fourth of July toasts, and threats of direct action.

Kentucky farmers had behind them both local political and newspaper support. The columns of the *Kentucky Gazette* and the Frankfort *Palladium* rang with resolutions, oratory, and shouts of nationalism. The very economic lifeblood of the western country depended upon access to the Mississippi; otherwise the rising system of agriculture meant nothing more than economic strangulation. Away in New York George Washington and Secretary of State Thomas Jefferson were alerted to the concerns of the West. First they dealt with the Genet threat, and then they turned to securing concessions from Spain. Kentucky was ripe for a violent outburst, if not a revolution. On 12 October 1795, Thomas Pinckney signed the Treaty of San Lorenzo with Spain. At best this was a stopgap agreement. Upriver farmers under its terms could navigate the Mississippi freely and deposit their produce for resale in New Orleans for three years, after which a new place of deposit would be provided. The Treaty of San Lorenzo did not satisfy rampant expansionists. There were too many diplomatic complications in the Old Southwest for the right of deposit to last. As the flatboat trade increased on the Mississippi and as the cash returns exceeded $2 million, Kentuckians became even more anxious about a permanent guarantee of a right of deposit.

The southern trade involved still other concerns. Crews of flatboatmen spent two to three months on the rivers at the mercy of currents and other hazards. Men who had handled the plow in the spring and summer were now called upon to man oars and rifles, and even to use their fists. In that wicked stretch of soil clinging to the foot of the bluff below Natchez they drank, fought, caroused with gamblers and prostitutes, lost their cargoes and even their lives. Waiting for them upstream were families and new crop seasons. The thousand mile journey home was far more arduous than the river voyage southward. It lay 200 miles through Louisiana swamp country to Natchez, 360 miles across the wilderness heartland of present Mississippi, Alabama, and Tennessee, and over the lands of the Choctaw and Chickasaw Indians. Then 200 miles more through Tennessee and Kentucky to the Bluegrass. The road was beset by hazards ranging from mosquitoes, snakes, and bears to highwaymen and treacherous stream crossings. The journey, made by horseback and afoot, took anywhere from twenty days to two and a half months. In all it required five to seven months to make the round trip to New Orleans. On 4 January 1802, Robert Barr wrote John Breckinridge that not a third of the Kentucky boatmen who went south ever returned to Kentucky. This seems an extremely morose estimate.

When Thomas Jefferson came to office as president plans were made to improve the lot of travelers on the road across the two Indian nations. On 12 March 1801, the postmaster general wrote Secretary of War Henry Dearborn that it was highly desirable to open and improve the Natchez Trace. One of his reasons was, "The produce raised in Kentucky and Tennessee for exportation is conveyed by boats down the Mississippi and the boats with the produce are generally disposed of at New Orleans, being found very expensive & difficult to navigate them back against the rapid stream of that river. The boatmen after the sale of their boats & cargoes return by the above mentioned route to their respective homes. The badness of the road is a great discouragement to such undertakings." Eighteen months later Thomas Fenton wrote Gideon Granger that upwards of 4,000 boats had descended the Mississippi in the past six months, each carrying twenty tons or more of freight. The year before 450 flatboats had passed Loftus Heights between 1 January and 30 June 1801. The Jefferson administration responded to the request for establishing the overland trail between Natchez and Nashville by negotiating treaties with the Chickasaw Indians in that year, and by locating and blazing the Natchez Trace. Five years later Congress appropriated funds for relocating and improving this trans-wilderness highway. And so by 1816 flatboats arriving annually in New Orleans numbered 1,287, up from 455 in 1806, and 1,049 in 1808.

The *Kentucky Gazette* regularly published commercial information. On 6 August 1802, it carried the report of the surveyor of the port of Louisville for the first six months of that year. Cargoes valued at $590,965 contained 841 barrels of apples; 7,971 gallons of cider, beer, and porter; 80 barrels of beef: 3,300 pounds of butter; 1,237 bushels of corn; 85,570 barrels of flour; 100 gallons of flax seed oil; 272,222 pounds of hams and bacon; 42,048 pounds of hemp; 55,052 pounds of lead; 2,485 barrels of pork; 342 bushels of potatoes; 2,399 pounds of soap; 2,640 pounds of manufactured tobacco; 503,618 pounds of loose tobacco; and 13,666 feet of planking. No doubt Kentuckians had taken advantage of the rather generous terms of the Pinckney Treaty by crowding into the Louisiana port each succeeding year with greater volumes of produce. Too, more and more Kentucky farms were being brought into production and the lands were producing much larger quantities of a much greater variety of commodities. As annual deliveries of goods increased, talk of the inalienable right to use the river grew more strident and westerners pressured the United States to act to set the rivers free. No one appreciated the problem more than President Jefferson.

The Mississippi had to be kept open, and New Orleans as a place of deposit had to be guaranteed by one means or another. The section of the San Lorenzo Treaty applying to this subject was too indefinite. In Kentucky the governor and legislators were acutely aware of the building crisis. Kentucky newspapers, especially the *Kentucky Gazette*, published lengthy editorial commentaries, letters to the editors, and almost endless resolutions and ceremonial toasts relating to the subject. The General Assembly memorialized the central government repeatedly and the Kentucky congressional delegation was showered with protests.

On 18 October 1802, when the Spanish intendant in New Orleans precipitately removed the right of deposit, he made no provision for another place of deposit as provided for in the treaty. So suddenly was the right removed, and without warning, that other Spanish officials and President Jefferson believed that the New Orleans official had acted on his own authority. (Later this was proved not to be so.) Fortunately 1802 was a rather poor crop year in Kentucky, and Morales had acted at the outset of the harvest season. Nevertheless his proclamation created a furious uproar among Kentucky farmers. On calmer reflection it became clear that Morales had not closed the Mississippi River and that farmer-boatmen could still ship their produce through New Orleans, though they could not land their cargoes in port. Thus was created a highly fortuitous situation of farmer meeting purchaser in a mid-river sale of cargoes. On November 1 the Kentucky General Assembly met for its biennial session. Observers believed that conditions were right for an angry act which could lead to war. James Speed wrote Governor James Garrard from New Orleans that the Morales proclamation sounded to him like a declaration of hostilities. He requested the governor to correspond immediately with President Jefferson about the West's attitude toward the crisis. By December Kentucky legislators had adopted a resolution which also asked the governor to inform the president and the Congress of the depth of feeling in Kentucky toward the Spanish proclamation. Pointedly the legislators resolved, "We rely with confidence on your wisdom and justice, and pledge ourselves to support at the expense of our lives and fortune, such measures as the honor, and interests of the United States may require." President Jefferson acted promptly by sending both the Morales proclamation and the Kentucky resolutions and letters to Congress.

While Kentuckians talked of organizing a citizens' army to go against Spain in Louisiana, the port of Natchez was in American hands and within reach of the seagoing trade. Possibly there was in the end little actual disruption of the farm trade south. In Washington the Morales act was but a disturbing incident in a much more significant international drama. American diplomats in Britain and France had learned of the secret transfer of Louisiana to France in the Treaty of Isle Defonso in 1802. Already Jefferson and the American diplomatic representative in France were in the process of negotiating the purchase of Louisiana. The purchase was completed on 30 April 1803, a little more than six months after the removal of the right of deposit, and fortunately before any overt incident had occurred in the West.

Acquisition of Louisiana opened an even wider world of economic and political expectation for Kentucky. The course of economic life in the state promised to be smoother and the possibilities of appointments to territorial offices for faithful Jeffersonians seemed unlimited. In the context of current emotions Henry Clay wrote to Senator John Breckinridge, 21 November 1803, that a threat of Spanish resistance to the transfer of Louisiana to the United States could be serious. Volunteers had been called for in Kentucky, Tennessee, and Ohio. Clay wrote, "Armies, Seiges, and Storms, completely engross the public mind, and the first interogation put on every occasion is Do you go to New Orleans? If all who answer in the affirmative should really design to go, Government will find it necessary to restrain the public Ardor, instead of resorting to co-ercion to raise the 4000 called for." Lawyer James Brown, however, was less impressed. He believed it would take the added enticement of 150 acres of free public lands to spark western enthusiasm and muster the 4,000 troops needed. But raising the militia for a march on New Orleans proved unnecessary. Spain surrendered Louisiana peaceably, and the port was again opened for free deposit.

Resolution of the Mississippi question was one of the most

important events in early Kentucky history. Certainly it freed the state's farmers to develop their lands as fully as soil and labor would permit. And it generated an optimistic nationalism which in time was to shape an entirely fresh political approach to both national and western problems. There was, however, more involved in agricultural expansion in Kentucky in 1803 than the freeing of the river trade route. Farm production quickly outran the available means of local fiscal exchange. A makeshift scheme of barter involving shaky credits, debits, land warrants, the swapping of commodities, and the exchange of limited amounts of assorted foreign specie proved inadequate to permit economic growth. Kentucky had no banks, no clearing house agency, and no established credit granting institution. By the turn of the nineteenth century this lack of a financial institution promised almost as serious economic strangulation as the threat of closure of the port of New Orleans. Ironically, there was ingrained opposition to the establishment of banks in the state. Backwoods farmers had no real understanding of the need for a banking facility in the promotion of their own welfare. Opposition to banks grew partly out of westerners' suspicion and distaste for Hamiltonian fiscal policies, partly out of the memory of the worthlessness of Virginia and continental currency and the uncertain fluctuations of notes, but largely out of the imagined economic power of bankers.

The promoters who successfully established the first bank in Kentucky on 16 December 1802 attempted to disguise their institution as an insurance company. Ostensibly the Kentucky Insurance Company was chartered to insure flatboats and their cargoes. It was said later that legislators were tricked into chartering the bank through incomprehension of the somewhat involved language contained in the bill, which permitted the company to issue paper notes. Basically nothing could have been of greater service to the rising agricultural economy than an efficient bank. The Kentucky Insurance Company charter, however, contained such a strong element of deception that the company was immediately involved in political infighting, and in 1805 an attempt was made to revoke its charter. In the meantime Kentucky continued to suffer for lack of liquid means of exchange.

By 1806 it was clear to even the most prejudiced mind that a bank had to be established to facilitate trade, and especially to get Kentucky drafts validated abroad. On December 26 the legislature chartered the Bank of Kentucky with a capitalization of $100,000, and on 12 October 1807 the necessary amount of stock had been subscribed and the bank began operation. The bank's establishment resulted almost entirely from the imperative demands of an expanded agricultural economy. Back of it was the rapidly maturing force and power of Bluegrass farmers as expressed through the leadership of the rising young Republican politician Henry Clay.

The land of Kentucky was productive. In 1817 Henry Bradshaw Fearon, a British traveler, was given a statistical statement of "the productions and wealth of Kentucky." The year before farms had yielded an income of $4,782,000, with flour, wheat, whiskey, and tobacco accounting for almost three-fourths of the total. Hemp, cordage, and bagging yielded $500,000; livestock, $300,000; pork and bacon, another $350,000. After 1815 and the introduction of the steamboat Kentucky's farm trade gained tremendous momentum. By that time the state's economy had been molded into a fixed pattern which would endure for a century. The pattern of Kentucky political, social, and economic life was cut to the lay of the land. No more eloquent tribute was paid to the land than that of Henry Clay, who wrote Rodney Dennis on 15 April 1849, "You do me too much honor in instituting any comparison between me and the renowned men of antiquity. I am in one respect better off than Moses. He died in sight of, without reaching, the promised land. I occupy as good a farm as any that he would have found, if he had reached it; and it has been acquired, not by hereditary descent, but by my own labor." Many Kentucky farmers in the nineteenth century shared this hosanna of self-satisfaction. Not one of them would have traded acre-for-acre with Moses or any of his children.

2

ARISTOCRATS
AND COUNTRY
COMMONERS

LONG BEFORE SETTLERS set foot inside the Cumberland Gap, the Kentucky region was destined to become famous for its livestock. The very trail the pioneers trod through the gap had been worn deep and smooth by the poundings of countless hooves of animals passing from eastern to western grazing lands. Throughout the region dense canebrakes were tunneled by deer and buffalo runs. The bold trails led from grazing grounds to salt licks, and all across the Kentucky country these saline oozes appeared as spreading pockmarks cropped and trampled bare by salt-hungry herbivorous animals. Felix Walker, a member of the Boone survey party in 1775, wrote upon approaching the future site of Boonesboro that, "On entering the plain we were permitted to view a very interesting and romantic sight. A number of buffalo, of all sizes, supposed to be between two and three hundred, made off from the lick in every direction; some running, some walking, others loping slowly and carelessly, with young calves playing, skipping, and bounding through the plain. Such a sight some of us never saw before, nor perhaps never may again."

Without doubt there came with the first settler inrush into Kentucky many hardy backwoodsmen who had clung to the outer edges of the spreading Virginia frontier as cattle grazers. Richard Henderson's colonizing party, which came up the Wilderness Trail on the heels of Boone's surveyors drove cattle and hogs with them. Along the wide wooded stretches the domestic animals had to be protected from depredations by wolves and panthers. Too, they had to be kept in check to prevent straying. The greater threat, however, was passing livestock over the fording places of the Cumberland, Rockcastle, and Kentucky rivers. One party of immigrants lost 500 head of cattle in a flood on the Kentucky River in the winter of 1779–80. It is almost a certainty that Benjamin Logan and his fellow pioneers drove both cattle and hogs to the Saint Asaph settlement late in 1775. From the headwaters of the Ohio migrating families drove cattle, horses, hogs, and sheep aboard rafts and drifted them to Maysville. Perhaps as many animals came over this route as came through Cumberland Gap.

Certainly all of the pioneers brought horses with them. These they rode and used as pack animals to fetch along at least the meager vestiges of a more settled civilization. William Calk's primitive journal is filled with details about the horses in his traveling party. In most immigrant groups there traveled that willful and self-sufficient pioneer, the rangy, long-snouted woods hog. Few chroniclers dignified this hardy traveler with description. His presence was noted at times by references to hams, bacon, and lard. Even the famous Kentucky riflemen were indebted to him for providing the greasy skin with which they wiped their ramrods and bullets. It is an anomaly of early Kentucky history that among the numerous atrocities committed by Indians against settlers, cattle, and horses there is no apparent reference to hogs as victims.

The hog which rooted its way through Cumberland Gap and up the Wilderness Road with human pioneers was a hardy beast. Slender-hipped and long of nose, the hog was mounted on tough, rangy legs which enabled it to dredge the woodlands for mast and bulbous morsels hiding just beneath the surface of the ground. It had no affection for its master and just enough regard for him to reappear on occasion for meager helpings of corn and salt. The hog took to the heavy deciduous woods and bluegrass plain as if it and its ancestors had always possessed the land. Sows bore numerous litters of pigs and the head count of hogs, so far as anyone could determine, increased enormously. These animals yielded meager returns, by modern standards, in both salt pork and lard, but by their very numbers they made an impressive contribution of provisions to flatboat cargoes and to trail droves on the way to market.

Whatever its status in the emigrant saga, the hog in time was to become a staple animal in Kentucky livestock history. F. A. Michaux wrote in 1802, "Of all domestic animals hogs are the most numerous; they are kept by all the inhabitants, several of them feed a hundred and fifty or two hundred. These animals never leave the woods, where they always find a sufficiency of food, especially in autumn and winter. They grow extremely wild, and generally go in herds. They are of a bulky shape, middling size, and straight eared. Every inhabitant recognizes those that belong to him by the particular manner in which their ears are cut. They stray sometimes in the forests, and do not make their appearance again for several months; they accustom them, notwithstanding, to return ever now and then to the plantation, by throwing them Indian corn once or twice a week." Michaux might have added that perhaps no other domestic animal so thoroughly conditioned the Kentuckians' diet. In fact ham has shared the center of popularity with all other regional foods and drink. As indicated by Michaux, corn was the most intimate link between the farmer-settler and his animals; likewise between the early Kentucky farmer and his land. Such great emphasis was placed upon the growing of corn in the earliest years of settlement that the act was accepted as a legal declaration of intent to remain permanently. Corn was a basic necessity both as human food and as food for horses and hogs.

In much smaller numbers flocks of sheep were driven over the trail to Kentucky. The wilderness land was not the most promising region for herding sheep. There were too many predatory animals, plus settlers' dogs, to permit safe grazing.

26

Also the region grew abundant wild nettles and burs which entangled wool beyond use. Michaux saw sheep on only three or four farms. The pioneers, he said, had little esteem for mutton, much preferring pork. Nevertheless it was an improvident immigrant who did not bring along in his baggage the necessary metal fittings for building spinning wheels and looms. These two domestic devices were prime necessities in fabricating clothing for families. Whether or not Kentuckians coined the term "linsey-woolsey," they certainly made capital use of the material in dressing themselves. Stockings, trousers, wide-flowing skirts, jackets, bed coverlets—all attested the presence of some sheep in Kentucky at an early date.

As Kentucky became more settled in the central counties, and pastures were cleared and turfed, sheep raising took on fresh impetus. The state was to share the national excitement over the importation of the fabulous Spanish Merino breed, which began in the early 1800s and spread to Kentucky by 1809. Thomas Jefferson had participated actively in the importation of the Spanish breeds. In Kentucky excitement over the new type was so pronounced that it was said that Samuel Trotter, a Lexington builder, contracted to construct the handsome home at the corner of Second and Market streets for three Merino sheep; but before he had finished the building the animals had become more common and the builder lost on the deal. In the great importation excitement the city fathers named a street in honor of the Spanish breed. By 1820 sheep raising had become fairly sizable, not only because of the Merino animals but also because imported English breeds were as popular and no doubt more practicable.

Unfortunately no contemporary journalist took time to write a detailed description of the contents of settler baggage, or to describe the full animal inventory of immigrant parties. It is known that along with each group of overland parties there traveled farm animals, herded by men and boys. These most often brought up the rear of forward patrols and of women and children. For some parties on the trails milk was a precious food supply, and after settlement venison was replaced by beef and pork.

27

In the history of its livestock development, as in that of almost everything else, Kentucky reflected a profound Virginia influence. In 1783, so it is believed, the first improved English cattle were introduced onto the grasslands of the Shenandoah Valley. A Virginian named Miller and a Marylander named Gough imported a shorthorn milking breed. This animal was more compact in conformation than the rangy, lightweight cows introduced at the outset of colonization or those animals which plodded up the Wilderness Road with the earliest Kentuckians. Virginians quickly became active in the cattle importation business, and their enthusiasm was transmitted to Kentuckians. Gough and Miller cattle were brought to the widening pastures of central Kentucky by 1787. The first animals were driven to Clark County by the sons of Matthew Patton and James Gay. In 1790 Matthew Patton left his Virginia valley home to follow his sons, James and Robert, to Kentucky. He brought with him a purebred Gough and Miller shorthorn bull, and a small herd of grade cows of both milking and beef types. In this herd came the famous bull Mars, which in time made almost as great a contribution to Kentucky agricultural expansion as did the human pioneers. Venus, the herd's purebred cow, like early immigrant human mothers of revered memory, lived only a short time after experiencing the ordeal of frontier travel, but delivered two bull calves which in turn contributed mightily to laying a foundation for a future cattle industry. Mars lived until 1806 and distinguished himself as progenitor of a revolution in cattle breeding not only in Kentucky but elsewhere on the frontier.

Engraved indelibly in the pages of Kentucky economic history are the names of Daniel Harrison, James Patton, and James Gray of Clark County. They imported the Virginia-bred English bull Pluto in 1803. West of the mountains he was bred to Patton cows with marked success in producing both milk and meat. In humble imitation of the rugged old pioneer Simon Kenton, Pluto in time was moved on to Ohio and the advancing frontier, where he again spread his fame in grade cattle production. William Smith of Fayette County imported the Miller-bred bull Buzzard in 1810. This animal, along with the famous Shaker, helped the farmers of Pleasant Hill in Kentucky and Union Village in Ohio to establish fine reputations as breeders of quality livestock. By 9 November 1817, the editor of the *Kentucky Gazette* could boast, "From the stock we now have, with proper attention to the keep and selection of males, we may safely calculate on producing as fine cattle as any in the known world." Editor John Bradford's burst of pride was premature. His editorial appeared on the eve of new and dramatic developments in the history of Kentucky livestock breeding.

Within three years Kentucky cattlemen were well on their way to establishing a major new breed of milk-beef cow and to writing a romantic chapter in Kentucky agricultural history. Expansion of pasture lands and the successful conquest of former canebrakes gave the central region an English grazing competency. These virgin pastures invited the upgrading of the animals that grazed them. The rising cattle industry in the first decades of the nineteenth century was impressive not only when measured in objective cash returns, but also since it became a highly cherished symbol of the advance of Kentucky agrarian civilization. Until 1817 all improved Kentucky cattle derived from Gough-Miller-Patton stock. But Lewis Sanders, an aggressive young Fayette County farmer, was captivated by stories of the fine quality and high prices paid for blooded cattle appearing in British farm journals. Immediately after the end of the War of 1812 he requested an English exporting company to purchase for him three matings of cattle of as many choice breeds. When the agent went to the country to purchase the animals he found cattle prices depressed and was able to add a fourth pair for Sanders's total $1,500 price. He bought Bakewell longhorns, Holderness, Durham reds, and Westmoreland longhorns—a fine assortment of the best British beef breeds. These animals were shipped to the United States by way of Baltimore under the care of experienced herdsmen. Unfortunately an accident at sea resulted in the death of one of the heifers.

While the exporter was scouring the English countryside to fill the Sanders order, Henry Clay entered the British cattle market. On his return to the United States from Ghent he stopped in London to attend a cattle show. There he saw prime specimens of the Hereford breed and ordered two bulls, a cow, and a heifer to be shipped to Baltimore. Peter Irving, a New York merchant, writer, and brother of Washington Irving, acted as his agent. The cattle were shipped aboard the *Mohawk*, whose captain was experienced in transporting livestock. Special stables were built below deck, and padding protected the animals against the roll of the vessel. They landed in Baltimore on 1 May 1817 and were turned to pasture with the Sanders importations. The Speaker of the United States House of Representatives visited the cattle in September and described them in a letter to Lewis Sanders. Almost with glee he wrote, the Herefordshires "are blood red without a particle of white, except the tip ends of their tails, most beautifully formed, somewhat of the symmetry of deer, smooth thin soft skins, but very small; indeed not so large as our native breed. Their excellence is said to consist in docility and nimbleness of the oxen of that breed, and the richness of the milk, of which, however, they do not give much." Within eighteen months he was advertising that his Hereford bull Ambassador was available for service at Ashland. These animals had as noble English ancestors as any humans who ever arrived in Kentucky.

The eleven cattle which made the long journey from England to Lexington helped greatly to advance cattle breeding in Kentucky, and ultimately in the West. Collectively they represented the improvements which had been made in English cattle. In their new pasturage these immigrants mingled their bloodlines with Gough-Miller-Patton stock to create the new strawberry roan, Kentucky shorthorns, which for many decades enjoyed popular esteem.

Throughout the nineteenth century Kentucky cattlemen imported both English and European stock, thus fixing firmly a lasting foundation for the western grazing industry. It was in this century that Kentucky gained the reputation of producing unusually fine cattle. The ancestral pedigrees of these animals read like those of aristocrats and doubtless are more accurate and reflective of selective breeding. Among the first illustrious bloods were such prima donnas as Lady Munday, Lady Kate, Lafayette, Napoleon, Ambassador, Lady Durham, Stone Hammer, and the royal red Lady One Teat. Owners of these titled animals were a coterie of Kentucky's best farmers. Among them were Henry and Green Clay, Lewis Sanders, the Reverend Thomas P. Dudley, James Prentiss, Jack Scott, Nathaniel Hart, and Charles S. Brent.

As tokens of their pride in owning fine cattle owners began displaying animal portraits along with those of family members. Edward Troye, the popular animal painter, enjoyed a comparable reputation with Matthew Harris Jouett, Joseph Bush, and other portrait painters. Troye painted a full-sized horse for sixty dollars, a bull for forty dollars, a cow for thirty dollars; and he made a special price of three or more paintings for fifteen dollars each. Perhaps the first "vanity" book ever projected in Kentucky was the one proposed by T. Campbell and Company to contain 260 pages with Troye paintings of as many animals. The publishers promised to supply each owner 400 prints of each subject included in the book. Drawings by other artists of Kentucky livestock appeared in the early farm journals; and in time separate volumes were devoted to bloodlines, achievements, and physical characteristics.

Set apart in both pride of ownership and human dependence was the horse. No historical record documents when this animal first set foot on the soil it was to make famous. Dr. Thomas Walker's exploring party in 1750 came mounted, and a year later the lone land scout and adventurer Christopher Gist rode across the eastern half of the state on horseback. Subsequently long hunters passed through Cumberland Gap to hunt and trap for skins and furs. At seasons' ends they packed their caches on horses and rode away. So natural a part did horses play in opening Kentucky to settlement that, like the thousands of faceless immigrants who comprised the trail parties, they blended opaquely into the story. During the hard years of Indian raiding, horse thievery was almost as much an objective as wreaking bloody vengeance on intruding settlers. No longsuffering pioneer came into the new land and endured greater hardships than did those plodding animals who bore burdensome packs westward. They trod treacherous trails across mountainous wilderness, forded flooded streams, and even faced marauding war parties of Indians. They came into the land without distinction of blooded ancestry or assurances of posterity, but these patient beasts bore the material trappings of Anglo-American civilization. Most important of all, these trail horses transported a small army of women and children to make new beginnings in virgin country.

As roads were cleared and village streets laid out, horse racing became a popular and rowdy Kentucky frontier pastime. It was at this moment that distinctions were made between beasts of burden and those dedicated to sport. The history of the latter is of a highly specialized para-agricultural nature and touched slightly or not at all the lives of masses of Kentuckians. By 1840 the horse population of Kentucky was 430,527, or slightly more than one for every two persons listed in the census count.

Throughout Kentucky history the horse has been the most popular farm animal, always enjoying a close affinity with its master. The mule was never able to loosen this bond, though it enjoyed its master's workaday respect for its capabilities at performing arduous tasks. There perhaps are few or no cherished Troye portraits of these animals, yet nothing caused a real Kentucky dirt farmer's eyes to glisten brighter than a well-matched pair of sharp-eared, fifteen-hand-high, sixteen-hundred-pound mules. Like their masters, mules had a fairly illustrious Virginia background, descending partly at least from offspring of George Washington's prize jack Royal Gift. In time livestock importers began bringing from Spain jacks and jennets to be used in the breeding of mules as domestic draft animals. Among the importers was Henry Clay. He perhaps would have had the "media" of today baying at his heels because he had a jack shipped from Spain to Baltimore aboard a United States naval vessel. Clay no doubt rationalized his official indiscretion by the fact that in time

32

from his Ashland farm went a numerous progeny to stock the southern mule market.

Before 1840 there had come to exist in Kentucky a rather distinguished ancestry for the Kentucky mule. Such forbears as Pioneer, General Gaines, Nick Biddle, Veto, Warrior, and Superior attracted admiring attention in livestock shows, along with the jennets Desdamona, Molly Madow, and Adaline. These too were pioneers who produced offspring of distinction. In the spring of 1839 John J. Hinton of Franklin, Tennessee, challenged Kentuckians to exhibit their prize jackasses against his vaunted King Cyrus for a fifty-dollar award, a challenge which went unheeded. Siding with the Tennessee Bluegrass mule breeder, the editor of the local Franklin *Review* taunted Kentuckians with the statement "We have greater jacks in Tennessee than Old Kentuck, if not so many of them, biped and quadruped."

Captain Frederick Marryatt, C. B., visited Kentucky in 1837 on his American travels. In Lexington he attended a livestock show and gave a firsthand account of this popular institution. "Of the cattle show at Lexington [Kentucky]," he wrote, "the fourth day was for the exhibition of jackasses of 2 and 1 year, and the foals of jennies also; this sight was to me one of peculiar interest. Accustomed as we are in England to value a jackass at thirty shillings, we look down upon them with contempt; but here the case is reversed; you look up at them with surprise and admiration. Several were shown standing fifteen hands high, with head and ears in proportion; the breed has been obtained from the Maltese Jackass, crossed by those of Spain, and the south of France. Those imported seldom average more than fourteen hands high; but the Kentuckians, by great attention and care, have raised them up to fifteen and sometimes sixteen. But the prices paid for these splendid animals, for such they really were, will prove how much they are in request. Warrior, a jackass, of great celebrity, sold for 5,000 dollars, upward of 1,000 sterling. Half another jackass, Benjamin by name, was sold for 2,500 dollars. At the show I asked a gentleman what he wanted for a very beautiful female ass, only one year old; he said that he would have 1,000 dollars, 250 for her, but that he had refused the sum." Captain Marryatt said mule breeding was a lucrative business in Kentucky and "I never felt such respect for donkeys before."

As southern cotton lands came under cultivation Kentucky mules became increasingly important to their breeders. In time mule drovers sought out purchasers among the new cotton farmers. During the latter three-quarters of the nineteenth century the mule trade grew in both importance and excitement. Out of it developed early a trading and swapping tradition centered upon spring court days. In some of the central counties "Mule Day" was far more exciting to county seat visitors than were the proceedings of the august magistrates. Some Kentucky horse and mule traders developed reputations for being astute bargainers and even sharper practitioners. Mule trading tested the gumption of both sellers and buyers, with absolute emphasis upon the principle of caveat emptor. Mule trading was often the poor man's sport, in apposition to horse racing and exhibiting blooded cattle.

Long before the earliest Texas longhorns were trailed northward across the plains, Kentuckians were driving their herds eastward and enjoying a prosperous overland drovers' trade. At the turn of the nineteenth century Kentucky cattle were driven to markets in Charleston, Richmond, Baltimore, and Philadelphia. Most of the drovers went by Cumberland Ford and Gap, where numbers could be estimated with some accuracy. In the winter of 1838–39 there passed over the river 4,549 cattle, 2,039 horses, 3,177 mules, 7,864 hogs, and 3,250 sheep—$1,780,426 worth of livestock. Every new decade saw an increase in the number of cattle in Kentucky pastures. By 1840 there were 787,098 head and twenty years later there were 835,059; by the latter date, however, there was less than one cow per capita for the 1,155,684 Kentuckians. Nevertheless, the cow was an ingrained part of domestic life, whether ranging rich Bluegrass farms, the rugged highland benches of Appalachia, or the Pennyroyal ridges.

Within a single generation hog drovers, or drivers, had reversed the march of the hog westward, and now headed him eastward to market. Early along the way from the Bluegrass to

Richmond and Baltimore, or to Charleston and Savannah, corn growers established feeder stations to supply drovers' needs. For more than three-quarters of a century Kentuckians drove their hogs into the southern cotton and tobacco country, selling farmers animals as they went. There are descendants of Kentuckians living in some of the Atlantic states who traveled into the region with droves of hogs, cattle, and mules, and chose to remain there. No less a person than Governor Isaac Shelby drove mules to South Carolina. On one occasion he called on the governor of that state in Columbia, and the two dignitaries spent a night drenching a "colicy" mule.

Like flatboatmen, land drovers were often rugged characters who endured soul-testing hardships to reach the cotton country. In Mississippi there are two villages, the Handle and the Skillet, which were old drover camps serving Kentuckians. The animals they drove before them may have been humble expressions of the pride of Kentucky; the drivers did not always appear to be such. Whether of Irish or Kentucky origin the ballad "Hog Drovers" is not necessarily wanton:

> Hog drivers, hog drivers we air,
> A-courtin' yer darter so sweet and fair;
> And kin we git lodgin' here, O'here—
> And kin we git lodgin' here?

> Now this is my darter that sets by my side,
> And no hog driver can get 'er fer a bride;
> And you kain't get lodgin' here, O'here—
> And you kain't git lodgin' here.

Originally the supply of salt was too limited and expensive to permit Kentucky hog raisers to butcher all of their stock to be sold in the form of salt meat, so that hogs had to be delivered on foot. Also, there were no other transportation means open to trans-Appalachian farmers. Early Kentucky hog breeders were the Shakers at Pleasant Hill. Most famous early private breeders were James E. Letton of Bourbon County, William R. Duncan of Clark County, Dr. S. D. Martin of Bourbon, and William P. Curd of Fayette. These breeders imported Berkshires, Irish Graziers, Woburns, Calcuttas, Chester Whites, and Essexes. Among the famous boars were Traveler, Dan O'Connel, and Sir Robert Peel. The sows were equally glamorous. There were Lady Peel, Lilly of Geneva, Donna Maria, Queen of Trumps, and Mrs. O'Connel. Many of the improved English animals were bought directly from the Duke of Bedford for Kentucky breeders, and J. C. Etches of Liverpool acted as agent for James E. Letton. In time these imported animals forced the rangy cane rooter deeper into the hills, and hogs from Kentucky rivaled blooded cattle and horses in fame. It was more important, however, that the new breeds produced three and four pounds of hams and bacon where formerly only one grew.

In 1840, a time when fairly extensive pasture lands were opened, the statistical profile of Kentucky livestock development could be reduced to simple human terms. A family of four members could have possessed a horse and a mule, a bull, three cows, a ram and three ewes, four boars, five sows and fifteen pigs, a rooster and two hens. This indeed was a generous stocking for an idyllic family farm, and with promising future prospects. In 1860, by comparison, 21 persons would have had to depend on a horse and a mule; 6½ would have looked to a single cow for milk; 2 would have had a single pig to satisfy their needs for pork; and 1½ persons would have fared better sharing a single beef cow. There was not enough wool in the twenty-pound fleece of one sheep to clothe 5½ persons. By the latter date both revolutionary changes and drastic losses of momentum had beset the pastures and stables of once proud Kentucky.

Hardly had the last gun been fired in the War of 1812 before Kentuckians began revealing organized pride in their blooded animals. The *Kentucky Gazette*, 27 May 1816, carried the momentous notice that there would be an exhibit of fine cattle, sheep, hogs, and horses at Lewis Sanders's Gardens at Sandersville just north of Lexington. Again the ingenious farmer was applying knowledge he had gleaned from English farm journals. As special enticement to local breeders to exhibit their animals it was announced that silver cups worth fifteen dollars each would be given as prizes. If not actually the introduction of the julep cup, the prizes marked the popularization of this prestigious Kentucky vessel in association with fine livestock. The cups were made doubly valuable when records of prized animals were engraved on their sides. These came to rest on family sideboards as status symbols of both choice drinks and fine quality farm animals.

This initial Sanders show brought together "the finest cattle in the state." Capt. William Smith brought his lordly sire Buzzard to compete with other noted bulls and cows of the Patton stock. There were sheep, "a good display of them" and a collection of hogs. The boar Calcutta was awarded a julep cup, and so was a flock of purebred Merinos. James Prentiss had his Merino rams sheared, even though out of season, and exhibited their fleece. Fifteen julep cups were awarded in this first cattle fair. The judges represented the early power structure of central Kentucky. They were Judge Harry Innes, Nathaniel Hart, John Fowler, Capt. Jack Jouett, of Revolutionary War horseman fame, and Col. Hubbard Taylor.

So enthusiastic was the response to Sanders's fair that a proposal was made and acted upon that a Kentucky Agricultural Society be organized. Isaac Shelby, just then retiring from his second term as governor, was elected president. For the next three-quarters of a century the agricultural society idea spread across the state as combinations of pressure, scientific, and social groups. It was through these organizations in the fertile central and western counties that prevailing agrarian sentiments were translated to governors and legislators. The collected documents of the General Assembly often referred to the agricultural societies as organizations to be respected.

Present at the Sanders show was Henry Clay, campaigning for reelection to Congress, Governor Poindexter of Tennessee, and R. Samuel Brown of Transylvania Medical School. Clay was confronting his opponent John Pope on the issue of his having favored raising the pay of congressmen. Here he could explain to an influential assemblage of Kentucky farmers reasons for his actions. The debate between the eloquent Clay and the forceful Pope, recently a controversial figure in the

War of 1812, caused almost as much excitement as the exhibition of fine farm animals. One other aspect of the show excited curiosity. Mrs. Edmund Long exhibited twenty yards of natural linen which she had woven. Miss Sallie Turnham exhibited an even longer bolt of bleached linen, and it was said she was the heroine who broke the sex barrier as an exhibitor.

Lewis Sanders moved away from Fayette County and the cattle fair was moved into Lexington and Fowler's Garden, where it became a major social event in which Bluegrass farmers paraded their families and blooded stock with equal pride. In the new location thirteen prizes were offered for exhibits which ranged from the best bull shown to the best hundred gallons of Kentucky distilled whiskey. The maker of the latter was asked to produce a satisfactory sample for the judges and a certificate of its place and manner of manufacture.

Proud families arrived at Fowler's Garden dressed in their fanciest clothes, and they brought with them ample supplies of their expert cooking. The loaded baskets they brought were said to contain prime beef, baked ham, fried chicken, leg of lamb, and stacks of pies and cakes. This was the beginning of the Kentucky State Fair itself, to which all Kentuckians were free to come with families, animals, fruits, and vegetables. Soon after 1818 fairs were organized in Bourbon, Mercer, Jefferson, and Franklin counties. These were to have long histories of livestock, horticultural, domestic arts, and culinary exhibitions. More especially county fairs became gay annual social affairs in which farm families competed against neighbors for coveted ribbons and prizes. The list of county fairs was expanded, and after the Civil War it was a poor rural county indeed which did not organize a fair. In fact the county fair enjoyed as much loyalty as did the emotional camp meetings of the era. At no place or time did Kentuckians express greater pride in the productiveness of their soil or the pedigrees of their livestock.

A reporter describing the Lexington blooded stock fair in September 1837 wrote, "We presume the world never exhibited finer lots of horses, cattle, jacks and sheep or hogs. We were there the first day, and saw the cattle. The sight made us prouder of our state, and we would have backed her against the world of fine stock, and spirited enterprise and emulation." Fred B. Bector, a visiting Tennesseean, bore out the local son in his immodest boasting. He wrote, "such an exhibition [of livestock] I should like to see in Nashville, but I doubt whether one so superior in anything, can be presented in America, or Europe even." Dr. S. D. Martin of Clark County went to the grass roots of the matter. He said, "in ten square miles of that county, in the year 1834, the cattle exported and sold returned to the raisers one hundred and sixty-eight thousand and three hundred dollars, besides sixty-eight thousand more for hogs, and the hemp and horse sales too." The total was more than thirty of the outlying Kentucky counties in that period produced together.

Kentuckians maintained their great livestock tradition through the end of the nineteenth century. The commonwealth never exceeded Tennessee and Missouri in the breeding and sale of mules, but it was not far behind. In time it lost much of its hog-raising status to the corn-growing states of the Old Northwest and its leadership in cattle raising to the western plains states. One of Kentucky's greatest tragedies was the havoc wreaked on sheep raising by vagrant dogs. For fear of alienating voters no governor or legislator has had the necessary courage to declare war on these bloodthirsty robbers through stern legislation.

Times have changed. Again emphasis is upon the growing of purebred cattle, and over a much broader geographical area. Purebred hogs are still prime farm animals in Kentucky, and country cured ham and bacon are in popular demand by even the most sophisticated gourmets. It would be difficult, however, to purchase a prime pair of matched fifteen-hundred-pound sorrel mules, almost as difficult in fact as purchasing a genuine Asa Blanchard hand-hammered, prize julep cup. Yet the powerful livestock tradition hovers over Kentucky as an aura of memories; not all of it is memory either.

There was romance indeed in Kentucky's leading men, socially and politically, engaging so actively in the importation and breeding of fine livestock in the nineteenth century.

These pioneers followed their own intuitions and used practical sense in their selection and breeding of better farm animals. They were, however, practical farmers with limited knowledge of the sciences of animal husbandry and soils. Thus it was that some of the momentum gained in the 1840s was lost and not to be regained until the rising era of the Kentucky Experiment Station in the first decades of this century. Scientists in the fields of breeding, control of diseases, horticulture, and land management enabled Kentucky to enter the new age with much more certainty than did the pioneers. The influence of the twentieth-century breeders and managers reached into nearly every area of human life in Kentucky. This influence appeared especially in the waging of battles to control the quality and purity of human foods, animal feeds, and fertilizers, and to outlaw contaminants, pollutants, and adulterations. This era of control, centered in the Experiment Station, reached even into that highly favored product of farm and distillery, bourbon whiskey.

In 1974 field crops yielded $918 million and livestock sales returned $669 million, with cattle ranking just behind tobacco in monetary value. Wherever two blades of grass grow in Kentucky there are cattle. In the Mountains, Bluegrass, Pennyroyal, and Purchase the hills are grass covered and host herds of Hereford, Black Angus, Charolais, and Simmenthals for beef, while imported Jerseys, Guernseys, and Holsteins in dairy herds supplant faithful old family milk cows.

Since the arrival of the Pattons and Gays, Kentuckians, like the children of Reuben and of Gad, have "had a very great multitude of cattle; and when they saw the land of Jazer, and the land of Gilead, that, behold, the place was the place for cattle." In the first settlement of the Bluegrass pioneer farmers, like the children of old, could proclaim Kentucky "is a land for cattle, and thy servants have cattle." The old line livestock importers and breeders went as far in the nineteenth century as unscientific farmers could go. Nevertheless they had set an enormously important example for farmers and livestock producers who settled the rest of western America.

3

UNTO THIS LAND
AND ITS PEOPLE

IN THE RICH Bluegrass region farmers and stock breeders early created an image of prosperity. At home and abroad they won a reputation for breeding fine livestock and growing abundant field crops. They were aggressively concerned about free access to the western river system, and ultimately they had significant impact on the political and diplomatic resolutions of western problems. The prosperous farmers and merchants of the central counties held the important national and state offices, imported purebred livestock, exhibited their animals and produce at fairs, and were visited by foreign travelers who came to the Ohio Valley.

There were, however, two Kentuckys: one which produced a commercial surplus of crops and animals; another which lacked easy transportation access to markets. That part of the Kentucky population settled in outlying areas clearly fell into the social and political category of the "great common people." Their churches were more primitive, their schools were late in being organized, no important press spoke for them, and no major political leadership sprang from their ranks. In the isolated areas circling the central counties humanity was willing to accept the fortunes of life as they unfolded, to cling to the old ways, and to block changes by creating stubborn barriers of social inertia.

The contrasts in the history of Kentucky are sharp. Involved in almost every phase of development of the commonwealth were social, economic, and politicial differences which had to be rationalized and compromised. While farmers on fertile Bluegrass soils measured growing wealth in crop surpluses which they shipped away to outside markets, subsistence farmers on poorer or more isolated lands were handicapped by lack of ready access to markets, varying qualities of soil, unevenness of topography, and poor local leadership in all fields. The timing of history itself played an active role in the sectionalization of Kentucky.

It is not difficult to trace the inflow of population into the central Bluegrass region and other fertile and readily accessible lands in the eighteenth century. Many immigrants left accounts of their coming in journals, diaries, and family correspondence. It is far more difficult, however, to be specific about the movement of settlers into Appalachia, the Cumberland and Green River valleys, the Pennyroyal, and the Purchase. Here the records of settlers more frequently appear in the legalistic forms of land entries, deeds, acts of the Kentucky General Assembly creating new counties, or grants of relief to certain groups, and in such other public records as court order books, tax assessments, and hundreds of thousands of court depositions. Occasionally a good family history gives an intimate and personal dimension to these regions, and sometimes authors of county histories have filled in many human details about original settlers.

Over the years some controversy has arisen about the origins of some segments of the Kentucky population. This has been especially true regarding the mountainous areas. From time to time overzealous regionalists have claimed that the highland Kentuckians were of "pure Anglo-Saxon" origins, and they have seemed to imply that there was a blood difference between the mountaineers and other Kentuckians. To accept this theory is to ignore some of the most important social and economic forces in Kentucky history. Every Kentuckian in the formative years was influenced by his relationship to the land, by accessibility to the outside world, and by the diversity of agricultural production. These factors, rather than the blood of origin, controlled his place in the history of the state.

The "seeding of democracy" in Kentucky, as Thomas Jefferson had idyllically conceived it, took place not quite as silently as the settling of the nightly dew, but almost as universally. Once the noisy initial scramble for land ended, ordinary settlers poured in and, like the local floods, sought economic and social levels on the "wild lands" that were left. This folk process created islands of settlements which developed into communities and ultimately into organized counties. The courses of rivers and creeks, the lay of bottomlands, and the roll of the more fertile ridges all drew settlers. In many a community in the more mountainous areas settlement inched up streams and mountain shelves concomitantly with the expansion of individual families.

Whatever peculiar geographical and environmental influences bore upon people in any given area, these facts have stood out. Much of Kentucky was rural to an extent that gave intense emphasis to the American term "country." Most of the state was isolated by land and forest barriers, and the local population was made up largely of yeoman farmers who tenaciously held on to the old ways in family relationships, economies, religion, recreation, and attitudes toward natural resources.

Few turnpikes ran through the subsistence farming areas, and the common country dirt roads were poor and indifferently maintained. Under an old Kentucky law which required men, aged sixteen to fifty, to donate so much labor each year to highway maintenance, much of rural Kentucky was left in the mud. Few, if any, carping English and European travelers visited the rural "settlements" to view with alarm the insidious influence of slavery, to criticize American manners, or to search out big blocks of fertile lands on which to settle immigrants. There were no livestock farms with fine pedigreed animals and no major towns or cities to invite outsiders. Thus masses of Kentucky yeoman farmers were left largely to themselves, except during election years when candidates for state offices went among them to solicit votes. A large segment of the rural Kentucky population was born and raised in highly provincial communities. Members of numerous families, they often settled near their birthplaces, subdividing original land-holds. Consequently they dangerously reduced their economic bases to the point of producing merely subsistence livelihoods.

One of the great contradictions of Kentucky history is the fact that as late as 1890 many areas of the state were still in forest, and promoters of the commonwealth considered the uncleared lands cheap and unproductive. They conducted rather vigorous campaigns to attract immigrants to the state, but almost without success. One of the most serious isolative forces in Kentucky's past was the fact that after the first thrusts of westward expansion the wave of emigrants moving from the East bypassed the state. Nathaniel Southgate Shaler wrote in 1877, "As a general thing, it may be said that the lands in this State are much cheaper than in any State north of the Ohio River. This is owing to the fact that, destitute of eastern communication, the State has hitherto had but small share of the tide of immigration of capital and labor that has poured past her borders to fill the favored fields of the far West." In many areas in Kentucky as late as 1900 isolated lands could be bought for ridiculously low prices, most of them under ten dollars per acre. In some localities the price of land had hardly advanced at all within the past century.

So far as Kentucky's public records can sustain general statements, the basic rural pattern was of small farmers who owned from 50 to 200 acres of land. There were, of course, those who owned more, but the average was low. Some isolated rural Kentuckians could be classed as large landholders, and those who possessed river and creek bottomlands were the more fortunate. First settlers built pole cabins. Then they and their descendants began the process of developing through the stages of more permanent "double" or "dog trot" log houses to more modern frame structures. Such homesteads expanded accordian-like with the arrival of new family members. At their hearthsides fountains of nostalgia for the simple common experience of life on the land bubbled up in rich memories.

Property deeds and assessment records of the numerous Kentucky counties and reports of the United States Census suggest that the material base of the yeoman or subsistence farmer was a narrow one. He owned, as a broad general average, no more than a team of horses or mules, two or three low-grade milk cows, a sow and pigs, a few sheep, and an assortment of fowls. In many counties in the latter decades of the nineteenth century remarkably few farmers reported ownership of wagons and carriages to tax assessors, and they laid claim to less than $100 worth of farm tools and implements. Earlier assessment forms curiously included a column for listing pianofortes; this column was distinguished in most counties by its blankness.

Farmers outside the more fertile central and Ohio floodplain counties grew approximately 30 bushels of corn per acre, and the great majority of them listed annual productions of less than 150 bushels. They grew gardens from which they harvested enough vegetables to supplement austere winter diets. It was common in many rural sections for cabin porch walls to be lined with long strings of shucky beans and dried fruits. Apples were packed away in ceramic churns with sulfur as a preservative. Rural Kentuckians, like the Irish, traditionally had great fondness for potatoes; they banked them in straw and dirt or stored them in crude ground cellars for winter use. It was an indifferent gardener indeed who did not grow generous crops of potato onions, which came up early in the spring, to give variety to the drab winter diet. Cabbages and other leafy vegetables were favorites. So were cushaws, squash, and pumpkins, which could be cut into rings and dried for winter use in the same way peaches and apples were preserved.

Pork was largely smoke cured, and the countryman depended upon early winter hog killings to supply meat throughout the year. Hog killing during the first freezing days of early winter was an exciting event. There is perhaps no warmer memory of rural life than that of the moment when fresh meat reached the table after hog killings. Many a Kentuckian has grown almost poetic about ribs and backbone, fresh loin, souse meat, sausage, and even pigs' feet. Hams and bacon were dietary staples. In some areas farmers grew sorghum from which they made molasses, and this sweet nectar has also stirred rich memories of cold mornings and hot buttered biscuits. Sorghum was supplemented on occasion by wild honey robbed from bee trees and cliff pockets.

The whole tenor of Kentucky rural existence was governed by the changing season. The positions of moon and stars, animal behavior, changing phases of the weather, and even the memory of ancient lore, such as observation of ember days, Good Friday, and dog days, all held country people in a thraldom of old folk beliefs. Animal and insect signs were respected. A heavy coat of fur, early hibernation, unusual bursts of energy by squirrels and chipmunks in gathering seeds and nuts, were sure indications of the approach of a hard winter. The width of bands on the brown caterpillars called "woolly bears" was thought to be a dependable gauge of the mildness or severity of future winters.

The general nature of land and forests nurtured a vivid chapter in Kentucky folk history. No matter how much pioneers boasted of independence and individualism, they actually enjoyed little of either. Traditionally Kentucky society and economy were folk based and accounts of common work were frequent. Clearings, deadenings, rolling logs, splitting rails, loggings, house raisings and warmings lent a rich human dimension to conquest of the land. Beyond workaday challenges, the woods helped to generate a sporting interest among Kentuckians. The early long hunters explored woodlands, wandered along rivers and streams, stalked salt licks, and followed animal trails. Once on the land, settlers continued this tradition of the hunt and of marksmanship as a manly art, and it still is associated with the sylvan past. Hunting, the sophisticated sport of horse racing, and the common log rolling test of personal strength, all have been links to the frontier past.

Up to 1890, fully three-fifths of Kentucky's rural population

47

lived in heavily wooded counties where conditions characteristic of the great American frontier tradition had lingered through four generations. Except for the more fertile central counties and those bordering the Ohio, where commercial agriculture and pastoral activities encouraged the clearing of the land, the state was still wooded. The forest had a decided impact on the course of Kentucky life. Its floor was a veritable storehouse of materials for the support of a subsistence rural economy. Few places on the globe produced a greater variety of herbs, shrubs, vines, and trees in such abundance as did woodland Kentucky. Almost all of these were used in some form as physical and psychological balms. For all seasons and for relief of all maladies herbal specifics existed. Ginseng, though not a specific in the American folk pharmacopeia, was from the earliest human invasion of Kentucky a natural commodity with high sales potential. Dyes, representing the galaxy of brilliant colors of Jacob's coat, were extracted from plants and minerals. An abundance of tannic acid in hardwood barks encouraged the tanning of leather and the making of clothes and shoes. Folk use and faith in the natural products of the forest formed a seamless web of cherished beliefs, superstition, and even quackery. Just as the woodlands contributed to man's toils and woes, they also supplied him with panaceas for his distempers, frustrations, tragedies, and boredom.

The floor of the Kentucky forest also yielded rich harvests of bulbs, roots, and mast for droves of ravenous semi-domesticated hogs. Both bottomlands and ridges generated browse and grass for sheep and cattle, and nearly always without their owners having to exert extensive efforts. Most important was the fact that at least eighteen varieties of trees of commercial quality were potentially a richer resource than was the mineral earth itself. A major tragic paradox of Kentucky history is the fact that, with its enormous forest wealth, the state developed no major wood-using industries and there was little or no history of such sophisticated craftsmanship as characterized the great forests of Germany or England. With annual laments the reporters who informed the Kentucky commissioner of agriculture of conditions in the counties recounted wasteful harvest of timber. Often they indicated that virgin stands of trees were nearing exhaustion.

In Kentucky's rural counties prevailed an almost inexplicable indifference to, if not blind ignorance of, the value of natural resources. Paradoxically a close affinity prevailed between Kentuckians and their woodlands. Most of them were huntsmen who prowled the woods by day and night in search of game and sport. The woods provided them with the basic materials for establishing and maintaining their rural homesteads. There were poles and logs for houses, puncheons for fortress walls, logs for outbuildings, boards and palings for roofs and garden fences, rails to enclose fields and pastures, and wood for fireplaces.

An overlooked chapter in Kentucky economic history concerns fencing. In 1879 it was estimated that, if the state's archaic fence law were strictly enforced, fencing croplands to keep animals out and enclosing pastures to keep them in would cost, in labor and materials, approximately $75 million, almost seventy times the state appropriation for the support of public education in that year. It was further estimated that 2 billion rails cut from 70 million prime rail trees were needed to fence Kentucky's 125,000 farms. Annual repairs, if made properly, required an additional 280 million rails cut from another 10 million trees. To fence Kentucky's annual field crops, which were estimated to yield $87,477,374, involved an annual cost of 8⅞ percent. Livestock of all sorts was said to be worth $25 million and the $10 million annual fencing cost was indeed top-heavy; in fact, so much so that fencing became a luxury item. "We keep a dead capital," wrote the Kentucky commissioner of agriculture in 1879, "in fences, rotting and disappearing more or less every year, greater than the value of our livestock for which the fences are made. The yearly loss to the State, by the use of this expensive luxury, *fencing*, is equal to more than one third the value of the stock raised each year."

It is little short of historical sacrilege to suggest that the all but revered institution of rail-splitting was wasteful. Nostalgic Kentuckians reminisced about their prowess with axe, maul, hammer, and wedge in splitting rails. But the post-Civil war critic of fence costs viewed the Kentucky scene of wanton destruction from another perspective. He brought under fire that ancient seasonal ritual of logrolling. No statistician has ever produced a cost analysis of this back-straining act which denuded hillsides and bottoms of forest cover. Historians have written of it with misguided nostalgia, and as a form of common working democracy in which neighbors turned an arduous task into a jolly drunken social affair. If the wasting of precious forest resources were symbolized in solid wood bedsteads, chairs, chests of drawers, and tables, and were reckoned in modern prices, the cost would be astronomical. Those logrolling, woodburning Kentuckians who have appeared in the softening twilight of history as heroic frontiersmen would suddenly take on the character of economic brigands. Again the belated warning from Frankfort: "In one half of our state timber is plenty and cheap, so the farmers in that portion can still afford, though not wisely, to waste it in fences or burn it in log heaps; but in the other half, timber trees are getting scarce and becoming very valuable, and should be protected before it is too late to save them for all kinds of future emergencies." To many a Kentucky farmer clinging to hillside acres, land and timber were cheap, even as late as 1920, so why conserve resources? No matter what the commissioner wrote about them in his book they went their own way. The book itself was read by fewer than one half of one percent of Kentucky's "dirt" farmers; there would be few changes in the old ways.

In all sections of Kentucky, except the Inner Bluegrass, countless yeoman farmers supplemented meager crop yields by logging their woodlands during summer and winter seasons. Historians of the state have written volumes about the exploits of pioneer heroes, the bravery of soldiers, the wit of politicians, and the rhetoric of preachers; but some of the most rugged of all Kentuckians still go unsung and unrecorded. These were gritty souls who rode bucking log rafts down from headstreams abreast of rivers and creeks swollen by flood waters. No one has fully portrayed these sweat-and-tobacco-stained Paul Bunyans in the state's literature, though

John Fox, Jr. wrote of them. And occasionally an old-timer had reminisced about the days when he and a slender party of logmen pitched headlong down a winding stream aboard an assemblage of logs with nothing but a stern sweep and a bow oar to bring it to bay. Not even the famous flatboatmen had so little control of their craft or faced so much potential disaster. The bunyanesque souls who drifted out of the Big Sandy, the Licking, Kentucky, Salt, Barren, Green, Cumberland, Tennessee, and Ohio rivers were wholly at the mercy of rampaging streams. As late as the 1920s loose-jointed rafts seasonally appeared on creeks and rivers. Earlier they were common sights before the famous "Craw" in Frankfort, Smithland, Valley View, West Point, Jackson, Cattlettsburg, West Irvine, Newport, and even Louisville. To keep them afloat and disentangled from rocks, sandbars, overhanging trees and brush, and out of suck holes and narrows, required the same kind of courage as facing an enemy in pitched battle. Generous amounts of chewing tobacco and moonshine liquor were needed to steady the nerves and buck the courage of raftsmen. Landing a flotilla of logs in a sawmill boom was by no means the end of the logging drama. Like earlier flatboatmen who drifted farther away to New Orleans, upstream logmen had to toil homeward over miserable roads and trails, lugging with them ungodly loads of equipment. And the cash returns for their grinding labor were barely enough to supplement their subsistence livelihoods from the land.

A still different breed of countrymen sought income from a traditional source. They were the more recent stock drovers who ranged the back country buying hogs, cows, mules, and horses for the New South trade. They lingered about court days, visited farms, and loafed in country stores plying their trade. Herding livestock southward over bad roads exhausted the last ounce of human patience. A colorful trader-drover of the eastern Kentucky hill country was "Devil" John Wright, friend of John Fox, Jr. He ranged the area about the headwaters of the Middle Fork of the Kentucky River, buying livestock and begetting children. He and others like him rode and walked thousands of miles to market, eating and sleeping under the most primitive conditions wherever night fell and sleepy flocks bedded down. In the end they too garnered only meager cash returns from their labors.

By 1890 the general economic pattern of farming was deeply etched in the rural life of the outlying Kentucky counties. Resistance to change was almost impenetrable. Special local reporters wrote to the Kentucky commissioner of agriculture that people in their neighborhoods could hardly be persuaded to throw away degenerate seed stocks that had come down season after season from those which crossed the mountains with the pioneers, and to buy new varieties. The same thing happened in livestock production. The scrub bull and the range heifer were as much fixtures as grandsires and grandmothers. In all phases of life rural dwellers had stubbornly clung to their peculiar institutions and conventions. For example, there was literally no one with gumption or modern perspective who believed the para-militia system of cutting and maintaining highways was anything but a rural farce. The system was riddled with favoritism and administrative loopholes. But few local foremen or officials relished incurring neighborhood enmities or endangering political futures for the sake of a few miles of muddy roads. Under the old system the roads were going to remain muddy no matter what was done to them. And in Frankfort an agrarian-minded legislature was not willing to invite disfavor by either levying adequate road taxes or assuming the burden of building and maintaining highways.

It was paradoxical indeed that while Kentuckians were unwilling to support a better system of road administration, at the same time, in the 1880s and 1890s, their ire was stirred by the mismanagement of the semiprivate turnpike system. It had become corrupt, discriminatory, greedy, inefficient, and completely out of date. War was inevitable. It came in the form of tollgate raids in which keepers were whipped and abused, gates were destroyed, and other forms of violence occurred. Eventually legislators and their constituents had to accept modern economic and social facts. They had to assume rightful responsibility for breaking the barriers of isolation. They came to realize that nothing worked more harshly against full development of Kentucky resources than a lack of good roads. It mattered little that soils were fertile and productive or that meadows were ideal for grazing; if produce could not be delivered to markets at a profit, then the efforts of improved farming were almost worthless. After the Civil War farmers in the isolated counties faced the same barriers as earlier Kentuckians who had protested so vehemently the closing of the Mississippi in 1802.

The economic profiles of some of the counties in this era reveal the inequalities of production and income. Hardin County in central western Kentucky had been settled early and by 1890 had passed through nearly every stage of the state's development. Its population had reached 21,304, and its isolation and rurality were clearly mirrored in its thirty-five crossroads villages where store backroom post offices were located. The county contained 330,775 acres of land, 60,000 of which still remained in woodland with 10,400 more euphemistically classed as "meadowland." The latter designation perhaps meant abandoned and exhausted fields which had been turned back to the stifling cover of sassafras sprouts and scrub red cedar. The land was said to have the low average value of $6.62 an acre, and assessments on much of it were even lower. Finally, Hardin County spent on services $9,384.50 more than it collected in revenue, thus placing it in that humble position designated by later state finance commissioners as a "pauper" county. Corn and wheat were principal crops in Hardin, and only 361 acres were planted to tobacco. The county's deficit condition carried with it a pride-blighting stigma.

By contrast Bourbon County in the Bluegrass had a population of 16,976, planted 2,228 acres of tobacco, and produced impressive surpluses of corn, wheat, and hemp as well as other crops. Hardin farmers labored just as hard to produce 481 pounds of tobacco on an acre as Bourbon farmers did to harvest 1,132 pounds. Differences in livestock income were much greater, even though Hardin had half again as much land in meadow as Bourbon.

Knox County on the pioneer Wilderness Road in eastern

53

Kentucky and Butler on the Green River in the central western part of the state were almost equal in size and population. Each historically had depended heavily upon corn and the small grains, with Butler producing more tobacco than Knox. Neither county had ever produced enough corn and feed grains to sustain its human and animal populations. The land in each county was valued in 1892 at approximately $5.00 an acre. Knox spent $18,157.33 more on public services than it collected in revenue; and Butler, $8,465.93.

As meager as these statistical samples are, they represent in some perspective one of Kentucky's historical agrarian problems. Land was cheap and undeveloped, but roads were too primitive for efficient and easy transportation of any possible surplus commodities to market. Revenue fell far short of public needs, and rates of assessments ran anywhere from 20 to 40 percent of true property values. In turn schools reflected the level of the general economy; more often than not they operated as starveling independent districts which offered hardly a "subsistence" education to children. Other services were similarly limited. In far too many counties progress came, if at all, at a snail's pace. In this era the Fourth Constitutional Convention drafted the present Constitution, and from such impoverished backgrounds came a majority of the delegates, always conscious of the limited capabilities of most of their home counties. It is little wonder that they wrote into the new document restrictive clauses which reflected far more clearly the conditions of the moment than confidence in future progress. Nowhere is the frustration of an agrarian society struggling to enter a modern American age more clearly visible than in the vicissitude that more than half of Kentucky's counties are helplessly locked into deficit economies.

In spite of a strong element of negativism, Kentuckians have cherished the rurality of their state. They have bragged of their rural backgrounds, have sung the praises of country cooking and foods, and have grown lyrical about the unhurried ways of the past. Kentucky's idiomatic figures of speech reflect the very essence of agrarianism. By another measure, the files of the *United States Postal Directory* all but document the longtime boast that Kentucky has had more fourth class post offices than any other state. Clearly there was no shouting for joy, no noisy parading or setting off of fireworks, when the Congress in 1896 enacted the law which created Rural Free Delivery of the mail. Nor was there a joining of hands with West Virginia when that service was begun on an experimental basis the next year. If there was Kentucky granger support for this type of modernization, then it arose among dwellers on all-weather roads in some of the more populous central counties.

There was in 1896 scarcely a crossroads or creek fording which did not have its country store and post office. Tattered flags above shabby little structures signaled the presence of branches of the all but omnipotent United States mail service. Like courthouses and county seats, these minuscule islands of communication exerted a peculiar kind of political influence. Every postmaster was politically favored by his appointment, and he was expected to bestir himself to help keep his benefactors in office. In thousands of ramshackle cubbyholes or corners of stores mail was gathered and dispatched to the "outside" world. It was delivered by lonely servants who made their way on mule back or foot. There were no admirers to cheer them on as heroic riders dashing from point to point and guarding their precious pouches with their lives. In their own plodding way, however, they were faithful to the poetic dedication of the mailman by withstanding storm, flood, cold, wind, darkness, and angry dogs. They went the famous commandment one better by venturing up and down slick mountain trails and defying threatening conditions which more prudent men would have refused to encounter. The "Star Route" mail carrier was truly a hero in overalls who helped tie all rural Kentucky to the rest of western civilization; but like the froe, the broadax, and the splint bonnet, he has passed from the scene.

Beyond their mundane function as way stations for mail delivery, tiny rural post offices were gathering places more popular than courthouse lawns, and a lot freer of inhibitions than church and camp meeting grounds. Few of their patrons actually expected to receive important mail. When they did get a letter it was likely to be a dun from the sheriff for taxes, a request from a stranded relative who needed money to buy a ticket home, or a patent medicine advertisement. Patrons ambled into post offices and stores for the more important business of hearing the news, passing on gossip, voicing sharp political opinions, or outbragging their neighbors. Here they could enjoy the company of other people on the most casual social terms.

Kentucky country stores were virtually synonymous with post offices. Few gathering places in Kentucky were so comfortable or inviting as the stovesides and front porches of the country stores. These were choice grounds on which to grow bumper crops of imaginary corn, tobacco, and sorghum cane; to brag about the pulling power of mules, the milking qualities of favorite cows, and the size of fattening hogs. Here were no restricted hunting seasons on running foxes and raccoons up and down every creek branch in the country. Ever present were the traders who offered to exchange knives, horses, mules, dogs, or anything else that could be pried loose and handed over. Gossip was passed on for fact. Tales of local tragedies were told, retold, and enlarged upon. Here bad news traveled with the wings of the wind, and each person's business was everybody's business. The very focal centers of civilization for thousands of Kentuckians were such pastoral microcosms as Budtown, Lily, Raccoon Bend, Little Cypress, Papaw, Maddog, Melrose, Odessa, Rosine, and Pitt's Point. In fact, the Kentucky section of the *Postal Directory* is also a glossary of the countryman's imagination, whimsicality, geographical consciousness, sentimentality, and personal ego.

Places known only to local inhabitants, the postal services and commercial drummers, collectively mirrored the tempo of significant portions of everyday Kentucky life. From opening time to closing these shabby forums were town meetings in session, and every subject of concern to someone was discussed, analyzed, and disposed of in summary fashion. So far as governmental problems could be reduced to simplistic terms they could be settled in the most direct manner at stoveside.

No issue was too involved for crossroads pundits to see through and around it, and facts were more often confusing than helpful in reaching solutions.

More to the liking of most countrymen was the relaxing environment in which practical jokers, pranksters, yarn spinners, braggarts, and even narrow-minded dogmatists functioned. It was a dull village which could not scrape up a bully or two who spoiled everlastingly for a fight, a handful of trifling human trash, an assortment of characters, eccentric and comical, all of whom in their own way lessened the tedium of country living. From time immemorial Kentuckians have cherished the anecdote and reminiscences of the past. Local chroniclers who were able to recall in colorful yarns what happened in earlier days could make claim to sagacity and mellow dignity.

In 1880 there were 160 country newspapers published weekly in Kentucky with a combined circulation of 333,000. Most of them were basically political sheets whose economic fortunes ebbed and flowed with the coming and going of courthouse politicians. Editors supported or decried office-seekers in the heat of local elections with the full realization that their papers' survival depended upon patronage in the form of county job printing and legal notices. Post-Civil War rural journalism produced stalwarts like W. P. and Ed Walton of the Stanford *Interior Journal,* H. A. Sommers of the Elizabethtown *News,* B. A. Evans of the Russellville *News Democrat,* Lycurgus Barrett of the Hartford *Herald,* and Dan and A. A. Bowmar of the Woodford *Sun.* There were scores of others equally forceful and well known whose editorial voices signaled political directions; reined up faltering officials; boosted schools, churches, and farm organizations. They gave voice to local pride in one column and uttered disdain for community indifference and failures in another. They commanded the proper adjectives for praising accomplishments and stating ideals for future striving.

Above all, country publishers printed the news—almost all the news that could be crammed into the local columns by matter-of-fact crossroads reporters. They printed obituaries with eulogies that robbed death of much of its sting. There were warm weekly greetings for most legitimate births, and most marriages were hailed with paeans of joy and ecstasy. Haunting white columns in locally newsless weeks made the editorial bed an uneasy one. It was then that humorous tales, stories of the vagaries of nature, pictures of big rattlesnakes killed in the locality, outpourings of camp meeting preachers, and even a good dog fight were blessed salvation. When these failed there was always the possibility of fussing at everybody—at the poor excuses for roads, the failure of farmers to diversify their crops, and the far-off and soulless trusts.

Occasionally country editors parted the provincial curtain sufficiently to allow a glimpse of news about national and international events—just enough to convince the reader there was a bigger world around Kentucky, but not enough to explain how the commonwealth fitted into the scheme of things.

The more sophisticated daily papers of Louisville, Lexington, Covington, and Paducah also attempted to reach out to rural readers with bi- and tri-weekly editions, largely made up in the format of the country papers. Their collective files reveal a consciousness of the inherent rurality of Kentuckians. They frequently published special columns on farm news, market conditions, and the latest information about new types of plants and livestock. Other columns attempted to keep sharp and vital the tang of the countryside, and especially the nostalgia which beset sentimental urban and rural readers alike. George Bingham of the *Mayfield Messenger* syndicated his "Doghill Paragraphs" in which he caricatured the reports of country correspondents. These enjoyed wide distribution and popular reception by rural Americans everywhere. Tandy Ellis, a master of storytelling and especially of the country yarn, captured the essence of rural Kentucky in his pieces in the Louisville and Lexington papers. None, however, so thoroughly tapped the deep vein of rural Kentucky lore as Allan Trout. His column "Greetings," which appeared so unobtrusively in a back corner of the sophisticated Louisville *Courier-Journal*, rang true in both note and melody. Trout greeted his large audience of "hot stove and store porch" readers with propositions, nostalgic reminiscences, and the unanswerable questions of people who viewed the universe through the inverted end of the intellectual telescope. In a mock vein of profound "barnyard science" which had no elementary tables or hard and fast fundamental laws, he and his readers raised and answered questions about all the trivial phenomena and ways of earthy country life. He called his crossroads correspondents and readers "ridge runners" and "apple knockers," and with tongue in cheek he related to them by looking back to his own origin in "rock and cedar" hill country. Trout captured and held his fellow "scientists" by turning the most commonplace countryisms into involved philosophical propositions of masterful obliquity.

When Allan Trout retired his doughty leathern doublet of rural columnist fell upon the shoulders of Joe Creason. In his career Creason never planted bushel gourds, distributed ginkgo seed, or brought tumbling back the sweet memory of country youth by bragging up Barlow knives; but he gathered and printed the countrymen's humorous stories, observed their whimsical anniversaries, garnered a rich harvest of folklore, glorified many an otherwise unnoticed human being, and convinced Kentucky legislators that they should distinguish the state's arboreal beauty by making the coffee tree an official symbol. On a much narrower stage Clennie Hollon of Williba combined keeping a country store with publishing his mimeographed *Poor Man's Journal*. From vantage points behind his store counters he viewed the disintegration of traditional Kentucky individualism as it was eroded by a system of welfare serfdom.

With the passage of time Kentucky was pitched headlong into the maelstrom of national economic and social change. The seeds of revolution came in small packets. For instance, burley tobacco was introduced into the state in the 1860s, and by 1920 it had almost covered the agricultural counties. By the latter date subsistence farmers had opened a new source of cash income by growing burley. Universal symbols of tobacco growing were the long, white, canvas bed stripes which made their spring appearances with the regularity of budding dogwood, and the rambling barns which stood in graying isolation awaiting the harvest time. The Kentucky tobacco pattern since pioneer days was a fairly broad one, and over the years it generated numerous economic and social problems. A series of tobacco wars, outbreaks of ruinous diseases, and regulatory efforts bespoke the pattern's militance. Nothing revealed traditional Kentucky wishy-washiness more than the political dealing with the Black Patch Tobacco War. Time, however, forced both state and national concern with tobacco problems, which resulted in the instigation of crop controls and marketing regulations—acts which were challenged by rugged individualists in quixotic efforts to forestall breaches of agrarian laissez faire.

On the land the tractor has replaced horses and mules. So unusual is it for a farmer to be seen grazing a hillside with a bull-tongue plow and a mule that he becomes a photographic subject for the front page of a metropolitan newspaper. He stands out as a sweat-grimed symbol of the honest yeomanry of a bygone age. The impersonal tractor and its jangling equipment can never tie man to the land in such sentimental affinity as did the mule and the hand-guided plow. By the same token, the tin can, the cellophane package, and the deep freeze may represent significant advances in dietary provisions and sanitation, but they are poor replacements for the long tails of drying shucky beans and a smokehouse full of cured meat.

Other old bastions have either been assaulted or destroyed by modernity. The country weekly newspaper in which the editor enjoyed oracle status has succumbed to advertising and bulletin board service. In winning their causes, the old crusaders destroyed their own base of appeal. They beat the editorial drum for good roads, and when Kentucky began breaking the great rural transportation barrier after 1916, the editors encountered new and powerful competition. When the Kentucky General Assembly in 1948 enacted farm-to-market highway legislation it knocked loose the last major prop of the isolated agrarian way of life. Pickup trucks with ever-present cattle racks, and stock sales barns replaced the old livestock drovers and county court market days. All that lingers on from earlier times are the special trade days in some localities when hucksters, swappers, hawkers, and peddlers gather to deal in the artifacts of the past. They come with bridle bits, hames, horse collars, trace and breast chains, wagon and hayrake wheels, and piles of rusting hand tools. There is furious if not large trade among Allan Trout's "apple knockers" and "ridge runners" in Barlow knives, but more especially in sweet memories.

Constantly on guard like angry wasps are the postmasters and patrons of fourth class post offices. With unsettling regularity rumblings are heard in Washington apparently signaling the disappearance of this institution which is the last stronghold of rugged rural Kentuckians. Threats to its existence bring congressmen and constituents alike running with petitions and angry protests. But wolflike postal officials in Washington remain watchful and allow aged rural postmasters to retire without replacing them. Lowering the wind-tattered and rain-stained flag over a country post office under these conditions means the death of such places as Drip Rock, Drum, Cane Creek, Cottonburg, and Pigeon Roost. With their going passes the focal center of lackadaisical rural Kentucky.

It is impossible to convey a concept of the depth of change in agrarian Kentucky without resort to elementary statistics. In 1900 there were 234,667 farms which averaged 93.4 acres. This number had dwindled by 1969 to 125,000, but the acre average had advanced to 128. Acres in cultivation had dropped from 21,979,229 to 15,968,000. More revealing of the depth of fundamental change was the fact that in 1900 Kentucky had a rural population of 1,679,506, and its urban dwellers numbered 467,688, or 21.8 percent of the total population. In seventy years the balances were tipped radically: 1,535,000 to 1,684,000, or 52.3 percent urban. Equally revealing, in 1970 there were only two Kentucky cities with more than 50,000 population and in and around the borders of Kentucky there were five standard metropolitan centers.

Kentucky farmers in 1974 sold $1,587,000,000 worth of

produce, but the value added by manufacturing alone was $3,636,000,000. Overall the capital agricultural take was less than 10 percent of Kentucky's total cash income. There remained the old imbalances between the surplus-producing counties and the subsistence ones, and in 1976 there were still "pauper" counties. In many ways much of traditional agrarian Kentucky was in a comparable situation with one of its venerable sons, Uncle Tom Lane of Baizetown in Ohio County. He kept stored in his corn crib two coffins in readiness for that day for his wife and himself. He requested that his friends lower his body into the grave to the accompaniment of country fiddle music and that they engrave on his tombstone the epitaph, "Here lies a man who ate up everything he made."

4

"BRINGING IN
THE SHEAVES"

HISTORICALLY KENTUCKIANS have had an English and
Scottish zealousness for their institutions. Church, school,
family, and counties have held their affections. Institutional
formalities and conformities have cut deep grooves in the rural
life of the commonwealth. Pioneers struggling westward
brought nothing more important to their future social conditions than the seeds of cultural organization. From the outset
embryo settlements had some form of religious expression,
and as congregations began to form Kentucky countrymen
built simple little church houses which served their basic
needs as temples of worship. The first cabins were hardly
raised before log schoolhouses, churches, lodge rooms, and
even debating society halls appeared. In towns like Lexington
and Danville debaters continued the processes so eloquently
begun in Philadelphia in the spring of 1776.

Debating early became a Kentucky art. In formulating two
constitutions in the closing quarter of the eighteenth century
Kentuckians engaged in an enormous amount of discussion,
much of it in private debating clubs. Running through materials published in the *Kentucky Gazette* is the bold suggestion
that western citizens suffered anxieties about the powers of
government. They wished to regulate the application of the
laws, to raise public safeguards against political excesses, and

to ensure an acceptable structure of government. Even greater than fears of government oppressiveness were visible doubts that the people themselves would act responsibly.

One of the strangest of Kentucky anomalies was the fact that whereas debaters orated themselves blue in the face about fundamental political principles, missing from the record is any discussion of public education as a fundamental requisite of freedom. The first two Kentucky constitutions remain silent on the subject. Public schools appeared to be as foreign to the thinking of the constitutional convention delegates as were the trappings of royalty. It took the passage of three-quarters of a century and a vital stirring in America to awaken Kentuckians to the need for establishing this fundamental institution.

Constitutional delegates, however, were from the outset conscious of the sanctity of freedom of religious worship. Their attitude stemmed partly from the famous Parsons' Cause argument, in which Patrick Henry first distinguished himself as an apostle of liberty, and partly from direct personal experiences. There were actually some Kentucky immigrants who once had been jailed for their preachings back in Virginia. Some of the Baptists who came as organized congregations were in a sense refugees of former official oppressions. So were many of the people described by John Taylor in his *History of Ten Baptist Churches* (1823). And no doubt many of the earliest Presbyterian immigrants vividly sensed the urgency of freedom of religious worship and practice, which was regarded by them as basic to all other freedoms.

From its earliest beginnings religious development in Kentucky had a distinctly rural cast. Lands west of the Appalachians were safely beyond the pale of formal church laws and organized bodies; certainly they were well beyond the clutches of the Established Church. Whether by synodical or associational mandate, early Kentucky churches, except for those in the islands of Catholic settlement, were largely congregational in nature. As late as 1825 the famous Timothy Flint, representative of the Connecticut Missionary Society, wrote of Kentuckians, "The people are eager to attend public

65

worship, especially when performed by strangers. This insatiable curiosity, the eagerness for novelty, which is so discouraging to the settled clergy, and which so strongly marks the American people generally, is a passion in this state. The people have an excitability and vivacity, like the French. Unhappily enthusiasm is likely to be fickle. It is melancholy to consider, that the ancient character for permanence, which our societies used to have, is passing away in all directions."

Flint notwithstanding, the frontier was a happy hunting ground for crusading missionaries and lay ministers alike. The westward advance of religion to Kentucky conformed harmoniously with social life itself. The state's religious history is as much colored by the impact of the qualities of the land as is its general economic development. One of the most dramatic religious incidents was the coming of the two traveling church groups which crossed the highlands in 1781 and 1782 from Fauquier County, Virginia. These approximately 600 immigrants were Baptist in faith and came under the leadership of Lewis and Elijah Craig, Captain William Ellis, Ambrose Dudley, and others. Singing gospel hymns, they filed through the mountains on foot, resisting hardship, expressing their continuing faith by trail campfires, and dreaming of the glories of the land about the head of Dick's River. In time these immigrants spread across Kentucky building churches and factories and settling farms. With seeming theological contradiction, they built almost on the shores of the Ohio in Mason County the marvelous little temple of Minerva which still stands. At South Elkhorn, Georgetown, and elsewhere they raised houses of worship.

Hundreds of country churches still stand as rugged weather-beaten monuments to earlier forms of social life. Some of these houses, like the old Mulkey Meeting House, glorified God by their simple beauty, while others slighted him in shabbiness and formlessness. The great religious fermentation at the turn of the nineteenth century gave a new emotional dimension to life on the maturing Kentucky frontier. Like a tiny yeast culture the earliest of the spiritual outpourings occurred in 1800 at Gaspar and Muddy rivers in

Logan County. A year later the contagion brought people flocking to Cane Ridge in Bourbon County; the unbridled excitement which marked this gathering bordered on intemperance. Perhaps throughout settled Kentucky there was a state of religious fervor and expectation. In 1801 the times were ripe for an emotional outpouring. A negative influence was the acrimonious political debate over state and national issues, including the disputed presidential election in which Thomas Jefferson and Aaron Burr were locked in contest. But Jefferson's elevation to the presidency fired the expectation that Kentucky was about to enter an age of social and economic expansion. In a positive vein, the Indian menace was forever removed from the Kentucky and Ohio River frontiers. Anthony Wayne's victory at Fallen Timbers, and the subsequent Treaty of Greenville in 1795, was fundamentally a Kentucky victory.

Contemporary observers of the Kentucky scene in the early 1800s sensed the fact that a psychological change had come over the people. Such leaders as Bishop Francis Asbury, William McKendree, and James McReady realized as much. They sensed an emotional hunger for release from former pressures and for making expressions of religious conviction. Kentucky yeoman farmers in these years knew the underlying satisfaction that they had won the first round in their conquest of the land and that the more fertile regions already produced considerable surpluses of various crops. This itself was reason for deep thankfulness. Firmly fixed in their minds was the certainty that God had favored the settler and his new country.

For the most part Kentucky churches advanced in lockstep with the agrarian communities whose social and economic colorations they reflected. The history of every denomination and church organization in Kentucky, with the exception of the Episcopal and Catholic churches mirrors the experience of evolving from primitive intellectual and social conditions. Most religious activities were synchronized with the seasonal calendar of farming. One of the most successful blendings of religious belief and agrarian economy took place in the communal Shaker societies at Pleasant Hill and South Union. So thoroughly agrarian were these colonies that they almost became private experiment stations for breeding livestock and growing crops. Almost every week was a time of vigorous and emotional religious expression for society communicants, and every crop season was a time of expectation.

Out of the Gaspar River and Cane Ridge revivals came the annual camp meetings which enlivened social life in western America. For almost a century and a quarter this seasonal religious phenomenon was a cherished revitalization of sagging spiritual life. One of the most pleasant public occasions in many a Kentucky rural community was camp, or protracted "bush arbor," meeting time, which happily blended a refreshing of religious faith for most Protestants and pleasant socializing. These annual festivals were intentionally timed to occur between "laying-by" of crops and opening of the harvest season. Clearly visible in the fields by camp meeting time was proof of the success or failure of a season of arduous farm labor. When crops were promising, and there had been good seasons of rain, countrymen's spirits were high and they were more responsive to evangelistic appeals. Otherwise they felt contriteness and were also open to the consolatory promises of religious conversion.

Whatever spiritual resuscitation camp meeting promised, people relished these annual occasions even more as times for passing on the news, engaging in agricultural and domestic gossip, and commentating on current political races. There was never a time during the year when girls seemed more willing to be courted or when, in unguarded moments, reluctant swains were more likely to find themselves involved in matrimonial entanglements. For those well past the age of romance the camp meeting ground was a fine place "to see and be seen." It was a veritable parade ground for both the vain and the scoffer. Too, in surprising numbers backwoods bullies and adolescent ruffians gathered on the outskirts to pick fights and disrupt services.

Besides camp meetings, thriving country churches were a highly centralizing influence upon their communities; at the same time many of them were divisive of local peace and

spirit. Like the camp meetings, the rural church functioned as partly religious and partly social in nature. It is hard to believe that at no time before 1900 did more than 35 percent of Kentucky's rural population belong to a church. Attendance at religious services, however, often represented an unusually high percentage of a local population. In the same way there were considerably more organized congregations than there were church houses. School houses and other public buildings served jointly as religious meeting places.

Only a few Kentucky country church buildings could accommodate more than half of the people who might attend special meetings. A well-publicized emotional evangelist gathered flocks of listeners with mixed motives. Some obviously sought to bolster their flagging faith, some hoped to be converted, and some came to be nuisances. It was not unusual for rural preachers to have to deal physically with bullies who attempted to disrupt meetings. Old pioneers like Brother James Axley and Peter Cartwright brought disturbers to bay with their fists. Even in this century old-timers recall church ground commotions. Often the fact that only part of an assemblage could be seated inside the house resulted in outsiders taunting insiders, and sometimes there were fights. In parts of Kentucky where community frictions resulted in feuds, church grounds sometimes were meeting places for enemies.

Baptist, Methodist, and Presbyterian, in this order, were the major Kentucky Protestant faiths. Baptists were present in a half dozen sects or "varieties." This Arminian or Calvinistic faith has deep roots in Kentucky history. Squire Boone, who joined his brother Daniel on two occasions during his long hunting years this side of the mountains, was a self-ordained Baptist minister of primitive faith. Baptists generally held a minimum of hard and fast doctrinal or organizational rules and adapted themselves readily to primitive conditions of both frontier and rural society. Every congregation was a law unto itself, and every orthodox and literal interpretation of the Scriptures was within the fold of doctrine. Early Baptist ministers were supposed to be "called to preach" through an emotional personal experience. They underwent no formal theological education or examination and no doubt in most cases they were self- or deacon-ordained. A majority of earlier country Baptist ministers were laymen who shared a common cultural and intellectual level with their congregations. They read and interpreted the Scriptures in the most literal sense, delivered furious emotional sermons, damned sinners with vivid epithets just short of swearing, and frequently taunted communicants of other faiths as misguided.

Doctrinal or factional divisions among Baptist sects often rested upon literal interpretations of the Scriptures cast in the experiences of the rural Kentucky population. Among the sects were the primitive "one and two seed" partisans, the foot-washing Hardshells, the Regulars, and the more sophisticated Missionary Baptists. Doctrinal differences among them often turned more upon social and economic experiences than upon learned theological views. Whatever the particular differences in beliefs and scriptural interpretations, socially the independent Kentucky Baptist country congregations were grass roots organizations which embodied rural social experience.

Well into the twentieth century Methodists were no less emotional in their preaching, or less positive in their doctrinal assertions and beliefs than Baptists. For them rural Kentucky was a fruitful missionary field in which itinerate circuit riders labored with zeal. The hoary old Wesleyan crusader Bishop Francis Asbury crossed the Appalachians many times to preach, to proselyte for new members, to ordain ministers, and to organize rural societies. Contemporaneously the seeds of Methodism were also planted and nurtured by Francis Clark and John Durham, Virginians, who organized a society in Lincoln County. The Kentucky Circuit was created in 1786, and Methodist missionaries early learned the facts of rugged life in ferreting out communicants on the Kentucky frontier. They dealt with any and all settlers, from the rowdiest to the gentlest. Riding from cabin to cabin, they searched for lost souls and read their Bibles, Milton's awesome works, and John Bunyan's pilgrimage allegory. Many of their long-winded sermons gave off sulfurous emissions. They rivaled Baptist prophets of eternal doom and counted a complete emotional rout a manifestation of victory. No circuit rider could leave a class meeting or love feast in good conscience unless he had brought most of his listeners to their feet shouting and confessing their sins in testimonials.

Basically the Methodists were opposed to slavery, and this created some problems for them in central Kentucky. Circuit riders, however, reached beyond this issue to communicate with country people about the greater question of spiritual salvation. No occasion, not even a country fair, could equal the excitement of a rip-roaring Methodist protracted meeting. In an especially vigorous meeting preaching began with the weaker "eight o'clock" fledglings and proceeded through the morning with the powerful "ten and eleven o'clock" fire-eaters "raising the roof." Love feasts turned into emotional outpourings which served the same function as the Catholic confessional, except that the sinner exposed his misdeeds fully in public.

In much smaller numbers Presbyterian missionaries, beginning with the famous "Father" David Rice, visited Kentucky early. This faith, with its doctrinal and organizational formalities, was not thoroughly adaptable to the informal rural mode of life. Consequently it failed to grow in numbers. Nevertheless it was a fairly rare county seat town in central Kentucky which lacked the elevated steeple of Calvinistic faith on its horizon. This steeple also symbolized a maturing commercial society about as much as it did a place of worship. The same was somewhat true of Catholic churches, which sprang up in rural communities about Bardstown, Lebanon, Springfield, and New Haven. In this region the church was the center of the social and economic community and held its membership in a cohesive body—a sharp contrast to other loosely organized rural church groups.

Kentucky historically has been a land in which thousands of country churches flourished. In 1850 there were 1,849 churches. The Methodists claimed a church congregation for every 1,854 persons in the Kentucky population; the Baptists, one for every 1,231; and the Presbyterians, one for every 4,366. Roman Catholic and Episcopal congregations were much less numerous. There were 4.91 churches for every 100 square miles of territory. In 1890 the number of churches had expanded to 5,555, with 229,524 Baptists of record, 141,521 Methodists, 92,504 Catholics, and 40,880 Presbyterians—that is, 32.85 percent of the current population of 1,858,635. Again mere membership enrollments did not necessarily represent the institutional strength and influence of religion in rural Kentucky.

Since the end of World War I and the rise of the new industrialism, and with the development of more highly organized administrative oversight of traditional churches, there have come to exist in both rural and country town areas various modern Pentecostal sects which in recent decades have supplied the emotional excitement abandoned by the older and more sophisticated faiths. These newcomers also subscribe to a satisfying literalness in interpreting and teaching the Scriptures. These institutions have risen by repeating the rural frontier process of adapting to the times and conditions of large masses of relatively unsophisticated people. It was in the ranks of some Baptists and Methodists and the Pentecostals that dedicated opponents of evolution found support for their crusade in 1925 and 1926. They actually reached into the halls of the Kentucky General Assembly in attempts to suppress the teachings of the post-Darwinian generation of biological and geological scientists.

Even the most casual visitor is made conscious of the large cemeteries located about country churches. But there are also literally thousands of burial places strewn across the Kentucky countryside well apart from churches. Land-bound Kentucky countrymen, like American countrymen everywhere, were faced with an urgency to bury their unembalmed dead, who had to be interred as quickly and as near at hand as possible. In more isolated areas where ministers were unavailable on short notice burials did not involve religious ceremonies. These could be held later when there was less urgency of time and conditions. People in some rural areas of Kentucky have

73

celebrated the coming of late spring by holding memorial ceremonies, and these belated "funeralizings" have been occasions for proselyting for church members and warming up sagging religious spirits.

In the latter half of the twentieth century when armies of Americans march upon the past in search of ancestors, the Kentucky country graveyard has become almost as much a tourist attraction as some of the state's more widely advertised landmarks. Annually, pleading letters pour through the mails seeking information about ancestral pasts which lie in abandoned cemeteries beneath faceless field stones, or under no stones at all. This is an emotional hold which Kentucky has upon some segments of the national population which in earlier years drifted to other states and cities.

The fact that less than a third of Kentucky's people have belonged to a church in no way lessens its centralizing influencing in the past. In the radical shifting of the rural Kentucky population since 1920, many church houses have been left empty of members or abandoned altogether, along with decaying homesteads, as memorials to a rural society which once flourished about them. This was "home" in the fullest manifestation of this endearing word. On homecoming occasions, or even casual visits, the country church is a door through which the nostalgic native can pass vicariously into earlier days and revive the precious memories of cherished human and family associations. They are places where the homing native son can still gather personal news, recall tenderly remembered incidents, and see some of the wrinkled and fading faces so familiar to him in his youth.

For Kentucky countrymen, who from their childhood attended rural church services, there have been no sweeter nostalgic sounds than a congregation swinging enthusiastically through ancient hymns which set many a sinner's foot on the path of rectitude. Old favorites culled from Watt's classic *Hymnal*, the Methodist *Song Book*, and more recent sources have remained popular. It would have been a hardened soul indeed who did not respond to the rhythm of "The Old Rugged Cross," "Beulah Land," "The Old Time Religion," "When the Roll Is Called Up Yonder," "At the Cross," and "Onward Christian Soldiers"; or who wondered if salvation was worth the discomfort of sitting on a crude pine-board bench listening to offbeat renditions of "Amazing Grace," "Rock of Ages," and "Just As I Am." All of these were good tuning-fork, country strap-organ songs whose rhythmic augurs pierced the inner souls of countrymen. Organists and song leaders, like many preachers, were untrained and taxed their talents to the outer limits in rendering the old favorites; congregations accompanied them with more spontaneous joy than musical grace.

No memory of the prospering country church of the old days is more tantalizing than that of the bounteous "dinners on the ground." These occasions challenged Kentucky's champion country cooks to bring forth brimming baskets of rural staples and delicacies cooked to countrymen's tastes. It was nearly as much a matter of pride for a rural matron to take home an empty basket from a church meeting as to have a beautiful daughter capture the most eligible bachelor at the "meeting." It was worth waiting through high-powered "ten o'clock" preachings just to gather about the long communal dining tables sagging with the largess of the countryside—a generous garnering of the "sheaves."

5

"PIT OF A FRENZIED COMMONWEALTH"

From the opening of the great settlement path through Cumberland Gap there have existed many "Kentuckys." In the more academic language of geographical determinists, the state has been as sectionalized as any part of the Republic. Essentially, Anglo-Americans who populated the numerous sections of Kentucky were of kindred blood and had advanced westward upon the land in a common phalanx. Later they were reshaped by environmental forces into widely differing regional cultures. From the eastern Breaks of the Big Sandy River southwestward to the "Mississippi triangle" lie four or five distinctive regions.

Where the soil was fertile and arable there early came into existence a rural gentry who looked proudly upon their way of life as Virginian and, back of that, English. From the more prosperous agricultural sections came early political leadership. Nearly all of the long succession of governors down to 1928 sprang from the soil, and a majority of them were successful tenants of the land. Kentuckians who gained national fame as United States senators and congressmen were most often farmer-lawyers from the fertile central counties, and personal names designating new counties were largely of Bluegrass, Pennyroyal, and Falls origins. Down into the second decade of the twentieth century almost the only place where the sectional ganglia were gathered into a common cord was under the dome of the Statehouse in Frankfort. There Mountain, Bluegrass, and Pennyroyal representatives came together in common, if unequal, purpose.

The deep gash of the Kentucky River across the state took millions of years in the cutting. From highland divide to valley confluence, the river hurled down millions of tons of earth to enrich its shoulder lands. Vital nutrients from the hills were transported to the "outside" to feed bottomlands and another way of life. The rugged palisades created by ancient floodings were in fact extensions of wandering cliff lines which surrendered reluctantly to the river rock by rock. These towering limestone walls drew down with them slender timbered mountain fringes. In sharp contrast, beyond the rim of the palisades rolled the gentle hills of bluegrass fields and swales on which was seated a self-annointed provincial aristocracy. This social enclave was leaven for the tempers of rugged countrymen gathered in Frankfort as legislators and state officials. The graces and traditions of human associations of the older section dominated the town. From Louisville and its clutch of Falls counties came representatives with more commercial perspectives than their colleagues. Beyond the great Muldraugh Barrier countrymen wandered in from areas in varying stages of development, including those from the Purchase, where settlement was withheld by political mandate until after 1820. Some of the older and richer western counties rivaled the Bluegrass in agricultural production and the sustenance of a prosperous way of agrarian life.

Distinctive sectional differences composed a varicolored tapestry of Kentucky social history. Before 1880 neither historian nor novelist had drawn into sharp focus the lines of clear contrasts in cultures, nor had they perceived clearly the social and cultural forces at work beneath the surface. Both classes of writers had readily recognized that the trauma of the Civil War had divided Kentuckians along sectional and personal lines. Not even the debate over slavery, grown warm after

1845, had drawn diverging lines so clearly. No novelist prior to 1880 had thought to plumb the depths of essential Kentucky socioeconomic forces. Mrs. E. D. E. N. Southworth wrote tepidly of life in the Bluegrass in her *Tempest and Sunshine*, but so superficially that she hardly jiggled the curtain on the local scene.

It was significant that both James Lane Allen and John Fox, Jr., early in their writing careers, felt the need to explore the social and historical labyrinths of their fictional locales in nonfictional essays. Each writer also groped for central factual themes around which to build future novels. Not until he had done this did James Lane Allen's portrayal of his homeland begin to lay bare the bone and sinew of a countryside thoroughly committed economically and spiritually to agrarianism. Making a round of New York publishers in 1884, he called upon Henry Mills Alden of *Harper's Magazine*. Earlier Alden had published the Kentuckian's poem "Mid-Winter." In their conversation Alden turned his visitor's attention away from more esoteric subjects by suggesting that he exploit the local Bluegrass scene as a writing theme. This was in the dawning of that golden age when regional authorship was coming into its own. The New England giants were passing away and American literary tastes were shifting to new locales with brilliant arrays of local color.

In the South a new generation of writers had outgrown the war theme. Among them were George Washington Cable, Joel Chandler Harris, Mary Noailles Murphree (Charles Egbert Craddock), and Samuel L. Clemens. Each was gathering a host of readers for regional stories. To date Kentucky was unrepresented in this budding sectional authorship, yet both its Bluegrass and Appalachian Highland sections were integral parts of the southern scene. The Bluegrass, with its sprawling hills, sweeping valleys, and inviting pastoral setting, formed a cultural island in distinct contrast with the arrested colonial socioeconomic culture surrounding it. Here an agrarian economy sustained a populace which emotionally was anchored in an Anglo-Saxon past, but which in actuality depended firmly upon an affluent land that could sustain a self-created provincial society.

Beginning in 1886 James Lane Allen published in *Harper's Magazine* a series of penetrating essays about the Bluegrass region. In conflicting veins of romance and realism, he portrayed his homeland as a rural society living by its own codes of genteel behavior and social responses. He was ever conscious of the fact that, "What one sees may be only what one feels—only intricate affinities between nature and self that were developed long ago, and have become too deep to be viewed as relations of illusions." There were generous romantic illusions in the Bluegrass, but they were frequently forced into the background by persistent realities largely fostered by the region's necessary outside associations. It could not exist a world apart, and certainly it could not remain detached within Kentucky itself.

The Bluegrass's maturing local colorist turned introspective to view his region at the moment when a tiny and starveling Kentucky Agricultural and Mechanical College sought to establish itself as a scientific educational force. In his essays on Bluegrass court days, county fairs, and homes, the young author sensed the fact that a historical hiatus had occurred between the glorious springtide of livestock breeding and the organization of the cattle fairs and agricultural societies in the 1830s. Somewhere the movement had lost momentum, as was true for society in general. In the field of art there were no successors to Matthew Harris Jouett to paint ancestral portraits, and no Edward Troyes to give artistic perpetuity to prized sires and dams.

Unhappily the post-Civil War years in Kentucky were socially what superintendents of public instruction called a time of stagnation. Ironweeds crowded out much of the romance and promise of Bluegrass meadows, and the appearance of burley tobacco as a cash crop introduced a new form of commercialism to the fields. Across the land, in meadows and along fence rows, the lowly hackberry crowded in among black cherries, stately blue ashes, and oaks. At many an entryway, said Allen, gates swung listlessly on rusting hinges. Even so there was still romance to be wrung from the nostalgic past, and in his future novels Allen wrote with unflagging affection for the land and its past. His descriptions were shaped by the moldboard of romance, drawn from and softened by everyday experiences, and tinctured with heavy dashes of nostalgia. The captivating roll of the Bluegrass was caught in Allen's books "Underneath the pale blue dome of the heavens," where "The Eternal Powers seemed to have quitted the universe and left all nature folded in the calm of Eternal Peace." No matter what changes occurred, the land remained the setting for the novelist's books.

In *The Reign of Law, The Mettle of the Pasture,* and *Flute and Violin* it was beneath the dome of the pale blue heavens that the author exhibited his characters and scenes. The land and James Lane Allen's provincial loyalties were never out of mind, no matter how far afield he wandered in basic literary themes. In *The Reign of Law* he published much of the formula of Kentucky rural life: "Parentage—a farm and its tasks—a country neighborhood and its narrowness—what more are these sometime than a starting point for a young life; as a flower pot might serve to sprout an oak, and as the oak would inevitably reach the hour when it would either die or burst out, root and branch, into the whole heavens and the earth; as a shell and yolk of an egg are the starting point for the wing of an eagle." The shell for the author was the narrowness of the human mind which the rich Bluegrass had nurtured, and the egg was its agrarian way of life.

Historically, the facts of origins could be simply stated, as James Lane Allen wrote in *The Bluegrass Region*. "But as I was saying that the old race qualities are apparent here, because this is a people of English blood with hereditary tastes, and because it has remained to this day largely commingled with foreign strains. Here, for instance, is the old race conservatism that expends itself reverentially on established ways and familiar customs. The building of the first great turnpike in this country was opposed on the ground that it would shut up way-side taverns, throw wagons and teams out of employment, and destroy the market for chickens, and oats." This was the realist Allen writing, but he obscured reality under a romantic benediction in "Homesteads in the Bluegrass." "In Kentucky," he wrote, "a rustic young woman of Homeric sensibility might be allowed to discover in the slow-moving panorama of white clouds her father's herd of short-horned cattle grazing through the heavenly pastures, her lover to see in the halo around the moon a perfect celestial race track."

James Lane Allen had created a deeply etched pattern for future Kentucky novelists in his persistent probing of the issue of origins and adaptations in what he called the "pit of a frenzied commonwealth" (or its converse social and political stagnation). His more youthful contemporary, John Fox, Jr., sensed more acutely the deep contrasts which existed in Kentucky's slender strip of American geography. Surrounding the world of James Lane Allen in crescentlike embrace were the Appalachian Highlands, worlds removed from the central region. Until the opening of the twentieth century this land held its population in arcadian primitiveness. In their Revolutionary-era flight out of the eastern valleys, these settlers had passed through a curtain of place and time which parted momentarily and then closed again. It was this phenomenon of history that intrigued Fox. Like Allen, he probed in all of his books for answers to questions about the mountaineers' origins and their responses to an environment of semientrapment.

Kentucky's image, as emblazoned across the nation in blaring headlines, was of a land stained violently by the blood of feudists and their enemies. The mountains appeared, even to people of the Bluegrass and to many legislators, in the primitive coloration of transported Scotsmen and Irishmen caught up in an ancient internecine war. In 1898 John Fox published *The Kentuckians*, a novel about highland feuds and social contrasts. Whatever merit the book may have had as a novel, its value lay mostly in an undergirding of facts gathered in Appalachia by the author. In the human contrasts he drew between "Rannie" Marshall of Fayette County and Boone Stallard of Appalachia lay a full world of time and men. The two legislators personified the substance of Kentucky sectionalism. Using the contemporary social and historical observations of Theodore Roosevelt, Nathaniel Southgate Shaler, geologist, and Ellsworth Huntington, sociologist, the young newspaperman viewed the mountaineers and their arrested civilization. In *The Kentuckians* Fox portrayed the pioneer migration into the hills as the rushing in of a primordial human tide which lashed the hills only once and left much of its subdued flood behind in eddies of settlements. He wrote in analogy that the mountain ranges "gave a little, as earth and water must when the Anglo-Saxons start, but only so 'You may pass over and on, but what drops behind is mine; and I shall hold my own.' "

The harshness of life in the hills and their narrow valleys shone through in the unvarnished personalities of Boone Stallard and his people. They had started life as backwoodsmen a century before, and "they had lived apart from the world without books, schools, or churches since the Revolution; they have had a century of such life in which to deteriorate." Mountain men had lived hard on their raw land, extracting from it rough subsistence fare. Locked behind the roll of endless and impassable ridges, and held prisoners along wild, rock-strewn creeks and branches, they could do no more than come to terms with the land. The impact of this hard condition was described in a conversation between Anne, the governor's daughter, and Buck Stallard, a convicted feudist and moonshiner. Buck protested against what he conceived to be a legal discrimination against moonshiners who attempted to dispose of their corn crops on the only market available to them. He told the girl, "An' say, s'posin' you had a field o' corn in some deep hollow. You can't tote hit out an', if you did, you couldn't sell nary a grain." The only recourse open was to peddle it in liquid form across the border in the Virginia settlements.

Like Allen, Fox found fiction inadequate to present the Kentucky mountaineers; there was too large a body of fact to be treated in this restricted manner. In 1901, a year when Kentucky was beset by unsettling incidents of feuding and the aftermath of the Goebel affair, he published his probing book, *Bluegrass and Rhododendron*. In this social document Fox undertook to describe the highlander whose "Present is past when it reaches him; and though past, is yet too far in the future to have any bearing on his established order of things." The ax and the rifle remained his principal instruments in assaulting the hills and his most dependable tools in lurching toward modern civilization.

Mountain homes, said Fox, remained one- and two-room cabins with walls of unhewn logs, clapboard roofs bolstered in place by boom poles tied down with hickory thongs or weighted with rocks, puncheon floors, and battened window shutters. In some cabins Fox saw iron cranes which swung out of fireplaces to receive pots for cooking food. Spinning wheels and looms were crowded into fireside corners, and hominy blocks and hand corn mills were still in use. This physical inventory contrasted sharply with the Bluegrass homes described in James Lane Allen's essay, "The Blue-grass Region of Kentucky." Whether either author ever looked into the United States Census Reports or not, statistics in those sources sustained the factuality of their writings. Too, had these authors read the annual reports of the state auditor, the superintendent of public instruction, and the commissioner of agriculture, they would have seen revealed the social and cultural profiles of their regions.

In the year *The Kentuckians* appeared the Appalachian forest was still "primeval, its riches unrifled, and its people of another age—for the range has held its own." Fox knew the ways of livelihood of the men of the hills, and in an eloquently descriptive essay he wrote of the process of harvesting the natural riches of the mountains. He described the ordeal of rafting logs down the Kentucky River and of weary men tramping homeward over arduous mountain trails. Throughout his novels the theme of unseen riches runs like a madder-dyed thread woven through a bolt of homespun. The land was rich, not in the Kentucky affluent agrarian manner, but in trees, soils, and minerals. There was, however, a deterrent chasm—lack of education, an archaic mode of speech, an emotional religion, a sensitivity about personal slights, and the limited perspectives of time and place. Contrasts were deep-seated, as reflected in the personalities of Chad and Major Buford in *The Little Shepherd of Kingdom Come*, or in those of Boone Stallard and "Rannie" Marshall in *The Kentuckians*. "These men of the mountains and the people of the Bluegrass are the extremes of civilization in the state," said the novelist. "Through the brush country they can almost touch hands, and yet know as little and have as little care for one another as though a sea were between them."

Allen and Fox set literary patterns for Kentucky which have largely remained intact despite changing literary tastes and rising consciousness of the social forces which shaped the people. Agrarian Kentucky, with its rising hopes and dampening frustrations, has ever drawn its authors close to the land and its people.

Elizabeth Chevalier and Robert Penn Warren wrote of the bitter harvest of two widely separated agricultural regions. In *Drivin' Woman* Elizabeth Chevalier penetrated the heart of two perplexing Kentucky problems—one of men and women laboring incessantly on the land to produce the so-called yellow gold of harvest season; the other of marketing the tobacco crop. Behind both problems lay the tortuous facts of natural fortuity; the seasons came and went, some bringing high hopes, and others leaving behind despair and desparation. Well beyond the bounds of Kentucky, men and times worked to create economic uncertainties. Along the Tuckahoe Ridge of Mason County, burley tobacco farmers fought the monopolies as best they could with limited public and political support. "Pinhooker" and monopoly agent bought the sweat, hopes, and even lives of men and families with an inhuman casualness which stirred violent passions.

In the Pennyroyal, and in only a slightly different time, men, women, and children bent weary backs in fields of dark tobacco. Markets for the product of their labors lay well beyond their geographical or political control. Year after year the crop fastened its chains of serfdom more tightly about their ankles, and the heartless monopolies locked them in grinding poverty with ruinous prices. Robert Penn Warren's *Night Rider* graphically delineates the fears and griefs of men who

84

were being wiped off the land of their origin. Yeoman farmers struck back in the "Black Patch War" in the first decade of this century. In the only way they knew to fight they attacked a distant foe through direct physical force and bitter threats of more violence. They unleashed the pent-up fury of men locked in mortal combat, thus adding to Kentucky's already sullied reputation for violence. Under cover of darkness and behind face masks, night riders brought Kentucky's agricultural and political systems under fire.

Royal monopolies, American trusts, soulless corporations, and inept and cowardly Kentucky politicians all stood in farmers' eyes as threats to a once proud social and economic tradition. *Night Rider* bared in fictional form the fears, suspicions, and hatreds of men bound in poverty to the single cash crop—tobacco. They could see little beyond the white-sheeted plant beds of uncooperative neighbors, of the next growing season, and of their own curing barns. In furious night charges "Possum hunters" left behind scraped plant beds as evidence of their enraged determination, which was still more tangibly impressive in the red glare of burning barns and tobacco warehouses. Welling up in the marauding night bands were all the ancestral furies of Scotsmen, Welshmen, and Irishmen, all of whom at some time had taken direct action against oppressors.

In Frankfort fear mingled with expediency. The burley belt smouldered at heart with the fires of revolt. The courts were castrated by intimidation of the night-riding warriors. In Frankfort sat a spineless governor who had reached office by an act of violence, but was incapable of positive action even had times been normal. Segments of the Kentucky press lacked courage to speak out against the excesses of vigilantism because they feared retaliation. Robert Penn Warren's *Night Rider* epitomized the unleashed emotions, the tribulations of the land, and the thunderous implications for all of Kentucky's agrarian way of life.

In even closer affinity with the land, Elizabeth Madox Roberts wrote in emotionally involved symbolism of the seasons and the earth. She created biblical and classical analogies in several of her books. Her emotional and symbolical progression embraced the very souls of the people who stirred her soil. In accurate settings she portrayed one of the most important social phenomena of the land—tobacco tenantry. Since antebellum years footloose farm workers had drifted wherever season and modest economic return led. With the war's end and the disappearance of slavery this tenant stream rose mightily.

The saga of Ellen Chesser in *The Time of Man* was that of literally thousands of tenants. Hope for these people was ever cyclic. Caught in social suspension, they wandered back country roads of no turnings and no recognized destinations. They bent their backs to set, hoe, harvest, and strip tobacco for bottomless markets. Like the farm animals where they squatted, they were important only in season. Their rewards were commensurate with their hopes. Living under leaking roofs and within soot-stained walls surrounded by musty reminders of the comings and goings of other wanderers like themselves, the tenants served their time. Ellen Chesser bore, physically and spiritually, the mark of tobacco tenancy as plainly as if it were a defacing birthmark on a cheek. In youth she searched out the courses of streams and the lay of the land as if she were an animal thrust into a new environment and needing to establish trails and calling stations. Almost by instinct she discerned the lines of demarcation and the deep suspicions between the owners and the tenants of the land. For tobacco serfs the cycle of time and season brought some moments of simple joy, but more of frustration and disappointment. For Elizabeth Madox Roberts's tenants roads led downhill through harsh realities. They experienced fleeting intervals of youth just turning into maidenhood before marriage, of hasty and almost loveless marriage, the birthing of children, and the eternal moving along backroads from one shabby tenant house to another. Always the next farm, like the children Ellen bore, had less vitality than the last.

Tobacco tenancy in *The Time of Man* and in Elizabeth Madox Roberts's other novels gathered in the end into composite burdens of anguish and defeat. When Ellen and Jasper

Kent and their children were one more time on the road under a cold moonlight, they ignored its turnings and asked not of its end. They sought only the security of a night's travel between one unsettling experience and the onset of another. Just as she had arrived as a stripling child in Henry Chesser's grotesque gypsy caravan, Ellen now rode wearily across the land, a spent human figure who symbolized the shadings of both the earth and the humanity which tended it.

Elizabeth Madox Roberts seldom ventured far from the familiar Kentucky soil she had known from her childhood in Springfield and later as a country school teacher at Maud. Her creation of characters and scenes, and of the outer turnings of human life itself reflect this fact. Often her humanity was cast in biblical, classical, and philosophical contexts. The fabric of her Kentucky land, the nature of its tenants, and the deep agrarian colorations were all softened by the interweaving of a dominant thread of the cycle of life itself. A furrow turned in her novels unfolded in the light and dark shadows of a wood-cut instead of rolling over in heavy earth-scented plates of gritty soil. Even her animals move with an undulating artistic grace.

With more profound realism, Jesse Stuart turned the furrows of his land in folds of a starkly earth-bound culture. In his *Man with a Bull-Tongue Plow, Head o' W-Hollow,* and *The Thread That Runs So True* he strode in lockstep with his characters across the countryside with the certainty of a man confident he had the choice of four trails by which to reach his destination. Never, like the Chessers, does Stuart take to roads in cheerless moonlight. For generations his people, like those described by John Fox, Jr., snatched meager livings from the land. Jesse Stuart's furrows, fence lines, and labors were but scratches upon an unrelenting land. Never could its occupants hope to equal or surpass the accomplishments of men laboring on more fertile Kentucky acres. Adhering to Fox's premise that the present was past when it reached his people, and that it extended far into the future, Jesse Stuart delineated the cycles of life in his hills and hollows.

Although he trod his native land with the soft step of affection, Stuart still brought that land under sore indictment, especially in *The Thread That Runs So True*. Perhaps oblivious to the interminable tables of educational statistics emanating from Frankfort, Stuart described the murky failures of vanishing, antique, one-room schools. He marched across his stage the names and faces of the pallbearers and mourners of Kentucky's public education tragedy. He wrote in eloquent, grass-roots terms of his state's agrarian backwardness. Innocently Jesse Stuart came to court as *amicus curiae* to those critical educational pioneers H. A. M. Henderson, J. H. Fuqua, Jr., M. A. Cassidy, and John Grant Crabbe. He appeared oblivious to the modern voice of James H. Richmond, who preached his cause so eloquently in his fervent address, "The case for the Public Schools," (1933). Stuart's strictures against his "pauper" county's schools and the petty politicians who strangled them was historically significant. It caught the old and confused agrarian flow of Kentucky life in a turgid channel of dejection, and just before the Great Depression crushed much of it.

Whatever their cultural and intellectual failings, Jesse Stuart's country characters were brawny, waspish, hospitable, rapacious, humorous, and stolidly resistant to change. He crowded them vibrantly onto the pages of his books, and, like Ellen Chesser in *The Time of Man*, they were caught inextricably in a web of tradition, recurring seasons, cyclical turnings of the land—and behind the all but impenetrable wall of geographical and economic isolation. Stuart's writings seldom ventured far from his native hills and hollows. The lives of people caught between mountain and valley frontiers validated his stories with the grist of simple experience of the everlasting struggle to survive. Nevertheless there was an undertone of destiny, of a creeping industrialism which drew men away from the hollows, tobacco patches, and crumbling homesteads, and also from ancient grudges, faltering institutions, and the spirit of the land itself.

In the broad sweep of the middle Cumberland Valley, people eddied in isolation, far removed from Kentucky's centers of industrial and commercial life, and from the "outside."

Seductively, the wages of Detroit, Hamilton, Dayton, and Cincinnati factories beckoned to them over the hard scrabble of the land. Like their forebears escaping from the uncertainties of older lands, the Cumberland dwellers, singly and in groups, drifted away to urban fleshpots. Farming as a way of life had failed them. For them time ran out when yeoman farmers and their descendants could no longer dredge subsistence livelihoods from soil and forest. The New Deal Farm Security Administration in the 1930s viewed this land as doomed. Subdividing of ancestral homesteads had reduced the land base to margins too narrow to provide for human existence.

Caught in the midst of darkening economic and social conditions, Harriette Arnow, a country school teacher in the middle Cumberland section, followed after her pupils who fled northward to the ghettoes of industrial Detroit. Far better than they, she knew the unsettling sociological and psychological adjustments these Cumberland people would have to make in order to exist in strange and crowded urban neighborhoods. In *The Dollmaker* she recorded their longings, their frustrations, and their grudging surrender of the ways of an agrarian culture. Few spiritual partings in American history ever drained so deeply the emotions of a people. Crowded tightly into urban streets, they were forced to forego dependence on many of their old and trusted institutions.

Like James Lane Allen and John Fox, Jr., Harriette Arnow went well beyond the limits of her novels and explored the Cumberland Valley in her searching *Seedtime on the Cumberland* and *Flowering of the Cumberland*. In these volumes she related her people to the land, the history of their entry, the making of settlements, and the exploitation of natural resources. Like their pioneering neighbors along the Upper Cumberland, the Kentucky, and the Big Sandy, the people below the falls clung only tenuously to the "outside" world by means of the fickle and sinuous Cumberland River. On its floods they floated their produce and logs to downstream markets, and they brought upstream far lighter tokens of Nashville and Bluegrass Tennessee culture.

Harriette Arnow's land mercilessly shaped rural life and destinies. Like Elizabeth Madox Roberts's symbolical cycles and turnings, life on the Cumberland included the ordeals of droughts, the sweeping destruction of annual spring tides, lack of education, and chronic economic deficits. Many Cumberland counties had long ago surrendered permanently to "pauper" status on the state auditor's books. Their institutions were starved, as described in the reports of county superintendents of schools and the commissioner of agriculture. Remote one-room school districts were trustee-ridden; schoolhouses were devoid of maps, globes, and charts, and were vandalized by patrons and petty politicians. It was from such schools and country churchyards that the people in *The Dollmaker* emigrated to shabby slum existence in the industrial towns above the Ohio. They were blood relatives of Jasper and Ellen Kent, except that their roads led further on without defined destinations.

Wendell Berry, like Kentucky authors before him, turned nostalgically to the land to give color and substance to his novels. There is a high fidelity, perhaps higher than in any other agrarian Kentucky novels, in his portrayal of the lives of men and land in *Nathan Coulter* and *The Memory of Old Jack*. In the lower reaches of Kentucky River ridge country, generations of tobacco farmers have experienced the same cycles of rural life. In cadence with the trees' spring budding and fall shedding one generation slipped away and another took its place. Just so, Wendell Berry touched his literary canvasses with an art derived from direct contacts with the earth and he depicted the succession of humans who served the land during the span of their lives, stirred its soils in season, made year-in-and-year-out physical sacrifices to it, and were jealous of their fleeting ownership and exercise of loose authority over it. These people sensed a peculiar joy, fell victims to accidents and grief, and passed on. As though it were a massive and permanent stage setting, the land remained in perpetuity, almost ignoring its transitory tenants and their efforts to mark it by their presence.

Wendell Berry's furrows are not the classicially shaped ones of gentler aesthetic tastes. His symbolism is not of vague ancient origin, and there are few or no subtle mystical turnings in the life stories of his characters. Like Old Jack, they all but stare out unseeing at the roll of the hills and their seasonal changes. His people are earth-earthy. Some have strange turns of mind and are preoccupied with halting approaches to their farms. They all made compromises in adapting to the ways of earthbound life. None rose above the status of rural yeomanry, and none, unlike Boone Stallard in *The Kentuckians*, left the land to run the political maze in Frankfort. None warred over the tragic economic plight of tobacco farmers, scraped neighbors' plant beds, burned barns and warehouses, shouted obscenities at "pinhookers" and monopolies, or fell victim to the courts. To them, however, tobacco was the soul of the land, a compulsive fact honored season after season by the breaking of beds, the setting of plants, cultivating, harvesting, and stripping. Thus life for the Coulters and Old Jack was orchestrated to the whims of the land and the seasons.

Over the long run of history hundreds of thousands of Kentuckians made compromises with life, lived out their allotted spans, and returned to the earth without ever having read a novel written about them. If they had they perhaps would not have recognized themselves as the characters. Nevertheless the spirit of the genre novels flowed out to them in second- and thirdhand accounts. Occasionally they picked up threads of knowledge of these writings in brief school terms or, later, from the racks of bookmobiles. If there has in fact been such a thing as a distinctive "Kentucky agrarian mind," then the commonwealth's authors have explored its corners in novels which consistently opened pulsating veins of nostalgia for older and simpler ways of life.

No Kentucky novelist has yet undertaken to draw the commonwealth's sections into a composite whole. Few have written of the agrarian political establishments and their transitory tenants—the men who have come from the land to make the public compromises necessary to sustain a vaguely defined way of life. Kentucky novelists have stuck with the mores of an agrarian society, honoring its ways and respecting its provincial commitments. Like Nathan Coulter's forbears and Old Jack and his kin, they have often surrendered to the passage of time and the unsettling impact of change. A decaying tobacco barn, an archaic man shambling along behind hand plow and mule, an aging couple whiling away their days on front porches, throngs of timeworn and sun-wrinkled men huddled in courthouse yards—all are survivors of Kentucky's agrarian past.

6

"THEY WILL ARISE
LIKE FIREFLIES
AT SUMMER SUNSET"

JOHN D. TAYLOR optimistically asserted in October 1849 that, as a result of writing an educational clause into the new constitution, Kentucky would in time be illuminated by the sparkle of one-room temples of intellectual light. A half century later Kentucky had become famous as home to thousands of one-room schools with hovering boards of district trustees. For the great mass of rural people these homely little structures became at once monuments to simple learning and symbols of limited opportunities. Like local churches, the schools were also focal centers of community life. For four or five months of split-school sessions they served rural youth somewhat as vistas into the fuller world of learning.

In time appeared rich clusters of sentimental ties to the schools. For hordes of unruly youth the shabby little schoolhouses also symbolized the heavy hand of stern teacher disciplinarians. Always there were pleasant recollections of childhood associations and pranks. Seldom, however, was there such emotional reverence for the country school as was felt for the neighboring churches. In a much broader sense the country school, functioning in its remote corner of land, reflected the tragic failure of the agrarian population to demand better opportunities for its youth. More important, public vision was blind to the fact that the creaking door of the schoolhouse was a portal to attainment of a better adjusted society and economy.

From the inception of the idea of universal public education, the collective state conscience was troubled. For a century and a half its people labored ponderously with the concept, always trying to soften two inevitable problems: financing schools as painlessly as possible, and persuading much of the population that education was both socially and functionally a democratic necessity. Nowhere in North America was the broad concept of public education more laden with conflicts and doubts. From the very outset of pioneer settlement a majority of rural Kentuckians appeared quite content to leave educational responsibilities to churches, privately supported academies, and a small body of concerned citizens. Many writers on the subject have concerned themselves with the history of educational beginnings in Kentucky, each new treatment opening wider the curtain of obscurity. Dancing against a shadowy background of fact and tradition are the forms of many individuals who made minor contributions.

Kentucky was tragically mislocated in both time and geography. One can only speculate what its cultural history might have been had it shared in the philosophy and substance of the Land Ordinance of 1785. One section of land out of every thirty-six square miles of territory would not have financed the establishment and maintenance of a country school for even a year, but at least the idea of public education would have been fixed as a state responsibility from the beginning, as happened in the states of the Old Northwest. Somewhat as a substitute to this federal plan, but more in keeping with the Virginia scheme, the Kentucky General Assembly in 1798 enacted the Kentucky Academy Land Grant Law, which set aside 6,000 acres of "wild lands" south of the Cumberland River for the organization of an academy in each county which sought to establish one. In time the more prosperous agricultural counties sought to establish these land-grant institutions, but with highly varying degrees of success. None of the institutions truly served the needs of the masses of country people, and certainly not those living in isolated neighborhoods. Just as the slender land grants provided in the federal ordinance were too meager to support schools, so the 6,000 acre Kentucky grants were insufficient.

Unhappily the Kentucky academy law set forth no practical philosophy or commitment to a system of universal free education. Rather it established, by implication at least, an unfortunate tradition of social privilege. Historically it was clear that delegates to two constitutional conventions and early legislators were unwilling to saddle the commonwealth with the necessary system of taxes to support effective common schools.

In spite of all the academic discussion of the great spirit of true democracy which prevailed in the councils which made Kentucky a state, there was no evidence that they considered education in any way a public responsibility, and certainly not an effective tool of freedom itself. In subsequent decades if governors and legislators had vigorously promulgated necessary tax laws and other legislation for the establishment and support of schools they would have confronted almost insurmountable obstacles. Land assessments were ridiculously low. In cheap land areas deeds failed to show the true number of acres contained within boundary descriptions, and always there was confusion about much of the ownership. Had there been full and accurate accounting of acreage and fair market evaluation it would have been almost impossible to organize and support effective schools in the poorer counties where, as late as 1890, the commissioner of agriculture reported average land prices were as low as four and five dollars an acre. The quality of social and cultural life in rural Kentucky communities was inextricably associated with land values.

No historian has yet fully explored the practical barriers to the development of a public school system in a purely agricultural state like nineteenth-century Kentucky. Though Kentucky's population grew phenomenally in the decades up to 1850, it was located in highly erratic community patterns, many of them isolated and detached from the rest of the state.

Somewhere in the early decades the concept developed that a public school district should encompass no more than four square miles, or 2,560 acres of land having a maximum market value of less than $2,000. Aside from this weak financial condition, in many a rural nineteenth-century Kentucky community it was nearly impossible to find enough children whose parents would voluntarily enroll them. More realistically, in many counties a district of twenty square miles would have barely produced a proper number of children for a school. Enlarging districts, however, would have placed schoolhouses out of reach of most children. Finally there was the all but insoluble problem of finding and paying adequately prepared teachers to hold four-month sessions of back-country schools.

A largely unsung early Kentucky political hero was Gabriel Slaughter, "accidental" governor from 1816 to 1820. He succeeded the tottering old military idol George Madison, who died after having been in office only a month. Slaughter was unable, because of his mode of elevation to the governor's office, to establish rapport with the legislature, and his modest statesmanship was wasted in his futile messages. He seems to have been the only state official during his term who had even slight awareness of the social fermentation stirring the nation following the War of 1812, especially in the neighboring states of the Old Northwest. Just across the Ohio River, Indiana constitutional delegates at Corydon, goaded by a small group of perceptive leaders, wrote into that state's first constitution a strong clause providing for a comprehensive and universal system of publicly supported education. Subsequently the new state's legislators accepted this mandate and made modest provisions for public schools. In Virginia, the source of cultural inspiration for Kentucky, Thomas Jefferson battled through the state legislature a program for establishing a public university. He argued that the capable common man, when educated, had the ability to become a constructive intellectual force in the maturing of Virginia's economy and society.

Governor Slaughter, whether or not he was informed of the Indiana and Virginia actions, voiced similar tenets. He suggested to legislators a system of free schools which would insure the education of Kentucky children regardless of the social and economic status of their parents. He proposed a sale of "wild lands," a revision of the law of escheats, and a tax on bank dividends to create an educational fund. These were somewhat revolutionary proposals for the times and they failed to secure legislative support. In 1817 he made the pertinent observation to tax-shy legislators that, "While the utility and importance of education is generally admitted, yet, either because the beneficial effects appear remote or universal, the subject does not seem to excite that lively interest and zeal which usually are awakened by the questions of local and personal character."

During the three succeeding decades some perceptive Kentuckians undertook to nurture the concept of education. Legislators continued to resist pressures to provide public support. Instead in 1821 they resorted to the weary Old Virginia dodge of responsibility by creating a literary fund. This at best was a hypocritical gesture devoid of honest merit. In fact, Kentuckians of this era willingly accepted a process of educational starvation. The meager documentary literature concerning education is cluttered with special reports, such as the provocative one made by William T. Barry's committee in 1822. This document contained an eloquently phrased argument against the tyranny of ignorance, and it was sustained by the inclusion of revealing letters from Thomas Jefferson, James Madison, John Adams, and other famous Americans. Legislators and citizens alike, however, were content to ignore the report—a costly public indifference.

When the Jackson administration in Washington had accumulated a capital surplus, Congress voted to return proportionate amounts of it to the states. Kentucky's share was $1,433,757, and this was sanctimoniously set aside inviolately as a public school fund. In its history, however, it proved too strong a temptation for grasping governors and legislators who attempted to destroy the obligation by obliterating its documentation. This fund in many ways proved an impediment to locally initiated fiscal legislation. Before Kentucky received the federal funds, the legislature in 1830 enacted a law which introduced an idea that in time proved to be infernal. Counties were authorized to create school districts in such numbers as they chose, to be presided over by cumbersome boards of trustees. For the time being Kentuckians rejected this law, but the concept of the petty district trustee system survived to haunt the state throughout the next century. There was other legislation, but none of it did more than reflect the fact that there still flickered a tiny spark of intellectual light never completely smothered by public apathy, ignorance, penuriousness, and political myopia. As a result four times as many Kentucky children remained without schooling as attended even indifferent classes.

These were only some of the more formal acts in the shamefully long struggle to create a system of universal public education accessible to all Kentucky children. The weak-kneed gestures made to date largely veiled the continuing Kentucky intellectual tragedy which occurred prior to 1908. So far as defectively gathered and recorded statistics are to be trusted, an unbelievably large portion of the commonwealth's youth was permitted to grow up in stark ignorance. The rate of illiteracy described by various sources was shocking, given a nation constantly changing from backwoods simplicity to urban and industrial sophistication. Had Kentucky enjoyed the prospect of becoming highly industrialized at any time prior to 1910, or had its more isolated rural sections enjoyed the promise of more prosperous agricultural development, a great mass of the population would have proved incapable of serving such an economy effectively.

In 1838, when vigorous personal efforts led to establishment of the office of superintendent of education, and when vigorous efforts in the more prosperous agricultural counties were being made to organize agricultural societies, the editor of the Franklin *Farmer* urged his readers to involve themselves in the state's modest educational crusade. He contended that better-educated farmers would be more capable of applying new methods of farming and livestock breeding. Besides, farmers should be as interested as professionals and urban residents in elevating their cultural and social status.

That year the legislature again enacted a law setting forth an outline for a public school system with provisions for a superintendent of public instruction, the organization of local school districts under the oversight of five trustees, and the selection of five county commissioners (superintendents). This was purely a bill of rural convenience. Louisville, Lexington, and Maysville were excepted from the law. In the pages of the statutes the plan seemed promising, but attempts to apply it proved inadequate. Schools were not organized; trustees, when elected, were incompetent; and Kentucky children were left to grow into illiterate adulthood.

Throughout the first half of the nineteenth century there sprang up perennial crops of rationalizers who delivered cliché-ridden orations and fallacious arguments. They at first contended that Kentuckians needed time to whip the Indians, to clear their lands, to build homes and towns; then they would turn to building schools. Once much of the land became productive there appeared partisans who advocated robbing the public school funds for capital to improve the rivers. Fervently, orators called upon the classics, the poets, and even the Scriptures to sustain their faith in education while violating their commitment to it. No doubt it would have been difficult to find a major Kentucky official before 1852 who would have admitted that he was not in favor of some kind of educational system. Yet it would have been equally difficult to single out one who would not have rifled the surplus school funds for noneducational purposes. Few would have voted an adequate tax program for the support of decent common schools.

Throughout the nineteenth century public apathy to educational progress was a stumbling block. Thousands of rural parents envisioned no real necessity for educating their children. They and their forbears had lived primitive lives closely identified with the soil. Their way of life was physical. Men wrested livelihoods from hills and valleys through back-breaking labor which did not require literacy. Nor were reading and writing necessary adjuncts to herding a drove of stubborn hillside hogs to market, bucking a willful log raft down a swollen stream, building a crude house, or marrying and be-getting many children. For the most part agrarian life in Kentucky eased forward in nature's grooves. Seasons came and went as God willed them, and if failure or disaster struck, then God had willed that also. Thus in the 1830s perhaps a majority of the commonwealth's citizens were untouched by the social stirrings which were occurring in the nation to bring about establishment of free common schools. In like measure they were oblivious to the phenomenal technological changes then occurring which in time would influence their lives. The greater mass of Kentucky farmers lived in ignorance of new farm implements. The century advanced to midmark with thousands of them still approaching their farming tasks in the archaic manner of their grandparents.

The educational movement in the early decades of the nineteenth century advanced on shaky footings. Though coura-geous crusaders after 1820 bore the guidon of public common education, they were also burdened with the issue of slavery. A contemporary observer wisely said there was "a malaise in the atmosphere of slavery," and nowhere was this more evident than in Kentucky. In picturesque prose John D. Taylor, a Maysville lawyer, said on 11 October 1849, "Did you ever, sir, in mid-summer, about nightfall, look upon a clover field and see fire flies rising out of it? Just so when the people had de-termined to have constitutional reform were our abolitionist friends seen springing up and giving light and hope to each other."

Slavery down to 1860 was a somewhat vague but forceful fact in Kentucky education. Some itinerate Yankee school-masters, traveler-visitors, and, after 1820, emancipationists and abolitionists were associated with the public school movement. For instance, it was not entirely helpful that the names of Calvin Fairbanks, Delia Anne Webster, John G. Fee, Calvin Stowe, and Horace Mann were both apostles of public education and crusaders for human freedom. After 1833 Kentuckians were highly sensitized over the issue of the fa-mous Anti-Importation Law. While this law and the abolition crusade were never directly associated with the public school movement, the slavery question had become so sensitive by 1848, creating such bitter partisanship, that no social question in the state could be entirely disassociated from it. In the rampant election to select delegates to the constitutional convention in 1849, Robert Jefferson Breckinridge, a major proponent for common schools, was defeated. He was an outspoken Presbyterian minister, and was thus suspect. Earlier David Rice, a Presbyterian divine, had raised embarrassing questions about slavery during formation of the first constitution.

Whatever extraneous forces worked against social advancement in nineteenth-century Kentucky, the moment for establishment of free common schools was long overdue when delegates assembled in Frankfort on 1 October 1849 to draft a third constitution. Some indication of the turn of mind among the hundred delegates appeared in the fact that there were forty-one farmers, thirty-six lawyers, and nine physicians. Too, it was significant that the subject of education was placed last on the agenda, occurring after a furious debate over slavery. The convention did not get around to discussing the educational report until December 10, ten days before adjournment. Delegates spent less than a day debating the subject, and no more than a half dozen of them took part in the discussion. The subject was introduced on the floor of the convention more as a flowery resolution than as the proposal of a fact-finding committee. Wording of the report clearly paraphrased that which appeared from the New Hampshire constitutional statement on public education. Copying the earlier documents, the Kentucky delegates declared, "The diffusion of knowledge and learning among men being essential to the preservation of liberty and free government, and the promotion of human virtue and happiness, it shall be the duty of the general assembly to establish within [four] years next after the adoption of this constitution, and *forever* thereafter keep in existence an efficient system of common schools throughout the Commonwealth which shall be open to all the white children thereof."

The florid statement touched off one of the most bizarre antisocial diatribes in Kentucky political history. The speech which "Kitchenknife" Ben Hardin of Bardstown made against public education almost stands alone as an American antiintellectual classic. By their silence other delegates reflected sympathy for the Hardin point of view. Throughout the constitutional convention there prevailed an agrarian timidity about asking future legislatures to vote tax measures for the support of any public activities, including schools. Too, there was an astonishing haziness about the definition of the term "common school." Some delegates were satisfied to resolve this matter by saying arbitrarily they wanted a system of "common English schools," but they gave no idea of what specifically they meant by the term. The debates revealed an abiding consciousness that any money raised by public means had to be derived from tax on the land itself. This was a highly sensitive political idea, adamantly opposed by the large farmer delegation.

It was with deep emotional feelings and justification that Ira Root, a Louisville lawyer, told his colleagues, "Would to God that the powerful talents of the gentleman from Nelson [Hardin]—for his talents must be felt wherever he shall take part—could have been exerted, at this late hour of his life, upon one of the greatest and most ennobling theatres, that would crown every other act of his honorable career." He then charged the venerable Hardin with resorting to a characteristic Kentucky country lawyer trick of telling crossroads anecdotes to obscure the seriousness of the state's intellectual crisis. He thought it certainly utopian to hope for a general diffusion of instruction across the commonwealth without the state's taking the initiative and extending aid to the school districts. Root said, "The raw materials exist in abundance for stores and factories, which all add more to the glory, the political and social blessings of a commonwealth than all the mules, jennies, and throstles that have been invented since the discovery of cottonseed. I mean, sir, the county school house. But it requires means to erect these factories of embryo statesmen, patriots, and divines, and means to keep the school master *housed*, not abroad." Unless the state supplied the aid, said Root, Kentucky children would continue to grow up in ignorance. "We all know that the wealthy themselves cannot in rural districts, from the size of their landed estates, and their consequent remoteness from each other, support a good school for any length of time, and that they have to send their children from home and board them near academies and colleges at enormous expense. . . ."

Kentucky's educational needs in 1849 were great. Larkin J. Proctor of Warsaw recited the facts that in 1840 there were 233,710 persons from five to twenty years of age; of these 1,419 were enrolled in colleges, 5,000 attended academies, and 24,964 attended short-term country schools. This left more than 200,000 children who had no access to an education and were left to grow into adulthood as ignorant as the hogs in neighboring woods. More than 40,000 adult Kentuckians were said by the Census Bureau to be unable to read and write.

John D. Taylor's patience grew thin in listening to the defeatist Hardin type of oratory in the debate on common schools. He exclaimed, "Great God, can it be possible that we shall be non-combattants in the great battle for life—for knowledge is life." He chided delegates that they could not adjourn the convention without acting positively upon an educational clause. "Will you throw over the sunshine of the heart a pall of neglected and violated social obligation and duty by your failure to protect and secure this fund [the surplus fund then held in escrow by the state] from legislative rapacity and duplicity?" Taylor thought that if the convention did act positively, "henceforth, under the new organization, schools are to spring up in ever neighborhood, and to be as free as the gush of waters from the mountain rock, . . . that they will arise like fireflies at summer sunset, giving life and hope to each other—light to the young, hope to the middle aged, and consolation to the old." This was indeed an idyllic vision of the force and power of free public schools. Tragically, mountains of resistance stood between the dreamer and the realization of his dream.

Following the debate, the constitutional delegation approved a vague educational clause which protected against rapacious legislative raiding of the bonded funds and any tax monies which might be accumulated. It provided for election of a superintendent of public instruction. But one reads the clause, the last active one in the constitution of 1849, in vain to find a direct and clear mandate to establish a universal system of common schools. It contains no implication of educational philosophy or even of direct concern, despite the fact that the educational committee had introduced the subject to the convention with the eloquent declaration that the diffusion of knowledge among men was essential to their well-being. The more than 200,000 educationally deprived children of Kentucky would remain, in the light of constitutional directive, in the state of ignorance to which they were born.

It took positive and aggressive personal leadership, and a liberal interpretation of the constitutional provision during future decades, to bring about the organization of a country school system which was to endure for more than half a century. Nothing in this period of history reflected more clearly the qualities of Kentucky's provincial, rural life. The struggle to achieve educational adequacy for the state was the most heroic of all the efforts of its people, even including the drama of its settlement.

Delegates wandered away to their homes in the far corners of Kentucky after the constitutional convention in 1849. Many no doubt believed they had served the commonwealth well by placing educational funds beyond the reach of grasping governors and legislators. Actually they had all but placed them beyond the reach of the schools themselves. It took a rowdy legalistic fight on the part of Robert J. Breckinridge to bring about the passage of enabling legislation to carry out the vague mandate to establish common schools. Governor John Helm, shortsighted and arrogant, vetoed the first legislation, but miraculously legislators overrode his veto. Breckinridge preached the convincing gospel that every Kentucky child had a right to at least a fourth grade education, no matter where he lived. It was easy to affirm a desire and expound a theory of social law, but its realization demanded herculean efforts. Qualified teachers were scarce, schoolhouses had to be built, and satisfactory textbooks must be procured. Local trustees, some of them opposed to universal education, needed to be indoctrinated, and county supervision had to be established. A contemporary observer said schoolhouses then in existence were "small, built without taste, and almost without form, on the most ineligible sites, very generally on the public roads where the children are permitted to gaze through little prison windows."

The gleam in the dreamer's eye was bright, but rising well above the Kentucky political horizon in the 1860s was the national crisis of civil war. Caught in an angry sectional squeeze for four years, the common school movement lumbered almost to a halt. A full generation of young Kentuckians was condemned to a lifetime of illiteracy. In 1865 hardly 20 percent of the school-age population knew what the inside of a school during session was like.

War's end meant the necessity to make new educational beginnings, but this time against substantially greater odds. Kentucky had lost manpower and property, and in the new era the children of ex-slaves would become an educational responsibility. Biennially for the rest of the century there gathered in Frankfort legislators who had little enthusiasm for financing education. One frustrated superintendent of public instruction declared it to be an age of perpetual stagnation and incompetence in the management of educational affairs. Niggardly legislators agreed to no more than token amounts of taxation, never enough to sustain schools above a poverty level.

Teaching a Kentucky country school prior to 1930 often required the wit of Solomon, the courage of David, the fortitude of Job, and the self-sacrifice of the widow and her mite. "Keeping" school was as much a test of physical endurance as of intellectual competence, and many a teacher proved to have neither. Even the best teachers were inadequately prepared and prior to 1908 had no place to turn for training. The so-called county normals were no more than farcical exercises in routine conducting of classes, exercising discipline, learning by rote bodies of unrelated facts, and cramming enough irrelevant information to pass an equally irrelevant examination. Perhaps there could be no satisfactory technique for teaching daily a multiplicity of subjects through four grades, during disgracefully short recitation periods in uncomfortable rooms, and with all grades huddled around a smoking stove. There was scarcely a country schoolteacher in Kentucky in the half century after 1870 who could not recite unpleasant disciplinary experiences. In some places the first qualification of a teacher had to be the capability of bringing the chief schoolyard bully and his sycophants to time. This meant whipping the toughest boy in school with a hickory withe or in a bare knuckles fight. It was also necessary to cajole cantankerous parents to behave, to serve as a confessor to aggrieved children, to endure all sorts of prankish indignities, and to tolerate interference from illiterate and overbearing district trustees. Teachers were expected to do all these things on "thankfully" received salaries of twelve to forty-five dollars a month for three- to five-month sessions. It was the practice in many rural districts to compensate teachers partly by "boarding them around." By this arrangement they were robbed of privacy, were often drawn into family and neighborhood rows, and accepted indifferent bed and board. They were handicapped further by the commonwealth's chronic failure to deliver funds to counties on time to pay salaries. Hard-pressed teachers were forced to dispose of their salary warrants at substantial discounts. So common was this practice that the legislature enacted a law making it an indictable offense for county superintendents to buy this distressed paper, a privilege which was reserved for shylock merchants and bankers. It could hardly be said with charity that teaching country school in Kentucky was the most inviting of professions. District trustees, even when honest and conscientious, were most often illiterate men who presumed to judge teacher qualifications, to interfere with teaching procedures, and to take sides in disciplinary disputes; more unscrupulous trustees demanded kickbacks for granting jobs. Always local politics affected employment, certification, and rates of pay.

Had there been no grasping district trustees, no quarrelsome parents, and no harassing playground bullies, "keeping" country school would still have had its major trials. That stern-voiced educator who continually lectured Kentuckians about their educational shortcomings at the turn of the century, James H. Fuqua, eloquently described prevailing conditions in the rural communities. There were, he said, 1,238 rotting log schoolhouses and thousands of shabby little plank buildings of lesser quality, and children in more than 2,000 schools sat hunched over their work on backless benches. Everywhere children shivered through intellectual cold "in the full blaze of the 20th century while searching for the long lost common devisor on a broken slate." Nearly 5,000 schools lacked globes, maps, charts, and all other teaching aids. The fate of these crumbling hovels of intellectual despair was controlled by 25,000 district trustees, most of whom would have been unable to distinguish a map of the state of Kentucky from a drawing of Mount Olympus. M. A. Cassidy of Lexington estimated there were at least 5,000 school officials in rural Kentucky who could neither read nor write, and twice that number who had no conception of their duties.

Thus it was that hundreds of thousands of rural Kentucky children and teachers labored through the "rule of three" while never having sat in an acceptable seat, drunk from a sanitary water receptacle, used any sanitary facility except the outdoors, beheld the shape of the American continent on globe or map, or even looked upon a chart revealing the physical make-up of their own bodies. Tragically, there were teachers incapable of using teaching aids even if they had been available.

Not only were teaching aids missing from the majority of the 8,330 district schoolhouses, but there prevailed the perplexing business of procuring suitable textbooks, and at a cost which parents could or would pay. A central problem in post-Civil War Kentucky was having enough copies of books for students to study from common sources. Often books, like outgrown clothing, were passed down through families. The necessary new books to meet the needs of a child in third grade cost less than a dollar at a country store, but many parents with six or eight children found this price exorbitant. Of romantic memory were the reliable old standbys: Noble Butler's *Grammar* and *History*, Webster's *Blueback Speller*, McGuffey's graded readers, and Ray's *Arithmetic*. In later years, and over loud protests, McGuffey's readers were replaced by the Baldwin series, also published by the American Book Company in Cincinnati.

H. A. M. Henderson wrote in 1874 that "Nothing, perhaps, has created more excitement during the year than the question of textbooks." The superintendent of public instruction was unrealistic to believe that in this age of beginning common schools Kentuckians would submit to the tyranny of uniform texts, especially when venal politics were involved in their selection. A decade later the legislature enacted the famous Chinn Textbook Act to regulate the choice of books. Aimed politically at the American Book Company, the Chinn act provided that the State Board of Education would list suitable books and that district trustees would make final selections. This arrangement was fraught with disaster, partly because many trustees could not tell for certain whether a book discussed the works of Shakespeare or the ice age in Tibet; besides trustees were ready targets for seductive publishers' agents. Superintendent J. D. Pickett commented in 1884 that in "The present age which teems with text-books," their selection was an important consideration. He advocated more extended terms of use partly to promote continuity in the "proper progress of the human mind," but largely "in the interest of those parents whose means are so limited that their children must necessarily use one after the other the same textbooks."

Over the years were enacted many ineffective laws dealing with textbook selection. In 1921 the Kentucky Educational Commission reported, "This zig-zag experience, capricious changing from one kind of machinery to another without genuine improvement, is fairly typical of the state's educational history." Lack of private or public funds with which to purchase books was doubtless highly deterrent to educational progress. Not until 1934 was this barrier partly removed by a public appropriation of $500,000 with which to purchase elementary textbooks. In all of the wailing over lack of educational progress in rural Kentucky, nothing reflected more clearly the emptiness of much of the educational process than a lack of books. Homes were devoid of reading materials and, sadly, too many parents could not have read them even if books had crowded their walls. Not until the post-World War II crusade to extend library services to all parts of the state was a raveling of this anti-intellectual binding begun. In a healthier vein, the ancient McGuffey and Baldwin eclectic readers did reveal to country Kentuckians that there was a literary world in which English and American authors alike gave substantial expression to human experiences.

Kentucky educational history cannot be presented in intelligible perspective without resort to at least some elementary statistics. In 1900, as noted above, there were still in existence 1,238 log schoolhouses; and in 1908 there were 739,836 school-age children, of whom 519,192 were enrolled in school, but only 311,922 maintained even a semblance of daily attendance. Kentucky spent little more than $3 million on its schools, including less than $1 million on furnishings and equipment, and less than $30,000 on library materials. There were 7,582 schools in 6,974 districts, and schoolhouses were valued at less than $1 million, or $132 per school. The latter figure was less than many Bluegrass farmers spent on a shed for a brood cow or a prize mule. This grim picture revealed the true cultural devotions of a people who asserted fierce pride in their homeland but refused to make the sacrifice necessary to improve their minds.

As unflattering a self-image as the above statistics presented, it took the thunderclap of two highly dramatic incidents to break the stupor of ignorance. The first of these was the "Whirlwind Campaign" of 1908 organized and engineered by the ingenious John Grant Crabbe, newly elected superintendent of public instruction. He conceived the clever idea of taking dramatic discussions of the state's educational plight directly to the people, even to those who could not read and write. For nine days in November 1908, twenty-nine speakers bombarded Kentuckians with the disturbing facts of the state's "ignorance and illiteracy" in preparation for action in the forthcoming meeting of the General Assembly.

In the ensuing legislature a series of laws was enacted which promised to revolutionize Kentucky education. Two teacher-training normal schools were founded, provisions were made for a high school in each county, the mode of teacher certification was revised, a child labor law was enacted, a compulsory school law was passed applying to towns and cities through the fourth class, local taxation was authorized, county districts were revised, and the door was opened for enactment of laws permitting later school consolidations.

The latter provision was long delayed in realization; roads had to be built, and the state tax broadened. Most important of all, however, the rural Kentucky mind had to be conditioned to accept ideas of change and progress. A second whirlwind campaign was conducted in June 1909. Crabbe's office supplied speakers with sheaths of data, including the statement that "There are more white native illiterates in Kentucky in proportion to the population than any of the Southern states, except those mentioned, notwithstanding that most of them lost more in life and property, proportionately than Kentucky. . . ." The press was flooded with releases describing Kentucky's lowly educational status and persuading the people to accept the new laws as means of relieving this embarrassment. These energetic campaigns went into every county, including two or three where no local arrangements were made to receive speakers. The year following the Crabbe onslaughts income from local taxation increased from $150,000 to $1 million. Thus a new age of public education in Kentucky was begun. In many counties mighty whoops of protests were raised against the taxing feature of the new laws, and there were other objections to drastic changes.

John Grant Crabbe was forthright in his public statements. In 1909 he wrote, "The real problem before the people of Kentucky is an improvement of our citizenship. This can only be done through better schools and more churches. . . . The

111

purpose is to get before the public some realization of the deplorable condition of our common schools in Kentucky and of our illiteracy and some understanding of the purposes and scope of the laws passed by the General Assembly, and also the fact that any defects in these laws proven by experience will be remedied."

One educational crusader in eastern Kentucky took the superintendent's statements seriously. Cora Wilson Stewart, as former superintendent of the Rowan County schools, and later president of the Kentucky Educational Association, had lived close to the stifling effects of illiteracy. In 1911 she opened a battle against ignorance by organizing evening or "Moonlight Schools" in which adult illiterates were taught to read and write. At the end of eight weeks she rewarded those who wrote her letters of appreciation with the gift of a Bible. This dramatic approach spread into other counties and caught statewide attention. In 1914 the legislature, in a moment of aroused emotions, hastened the enactment of a law creating the Kentucky Illiteracy Commission. It was said that in six years 130,000 people had been taught to read and write well enough to sign their names to legal papers. The "Moonlight Schools" by no means broke the back of illiteracy, but they stirred public awareness that such a disgraceful blight was costly to the state.

Again, in the midst of crusading fervor, war disrupted the educational transition. This time, however, World War I and its deep-seated changes moved Kentucky forward, maybe against its will. Federal highway legislation and the resulting good roads movement, the dawning of a new age of science, the rise of industries, and a shifting of population away from farms to urban communities made education more necessary than at any time in Kentucky history.

In 1920 Kentucky, statistically at least, had begun a slow but discernible departure from the past. Its school sessions, however, still averaged only five months, fewer than half its children maintained an average daily attendance, and the newly enacted compulsory attendance law proved almost impossible to enforce. Fourteen percent of the male voting population was still illiterate, as was 12 percent of the entire population. The state was low in nearly every category of national educational achievement, thus comparing intolerably with the shabby ground of the poorest of the lower southern states. In microcosmic sampling, Greenup County in 1932, the year of publication of Jesse Stuart's *The Thread That Runs So True*, received $10,000 more educational funds from the state than it raised by local taxation. Schools were in session less than four months, teachers were paid an average of $459.00, students attended no more than a fourth of the teaching days, and overall the county lost forever 50,000 precious instructional days. This miserable record was compounded by the fact that there were still 1,296 illiterate adults in the population of 24,454 souls. Repeated at least sixty times over in the so-called pauper counties, Greenup's condition outlined the necessity for a second and even more vigorous educational crusade following the end of the Great Depression.

Gradually more than 8,000 dilapidated one-room schoolhouses surrendered to consolidation and settled into the obliterating dust of decay or became even shabbier tenant houses and hay mows. District trustees thankfully surrendered to the fate of all flesh and were followed into oblivion by second- and third-class certified teachers who had brought to learning limited wisdom and less vision. Some fondness for the old days lingered in the memories of rural adults. But they bore the crippling traces of intellectual and spiritual denial by a society which proved both too penurious and too incapable of rising to the challenge of making Kentucky a more fulfilling place. Thus the cherished "western Eden" failed them at a time when mere physical existence was not enough to adapt human beings to the changing conditions of the land. The old habits of a century and a half of rural denial were deeply ingrained, and it took enormous expenditures of money and human ingenuity to correct them. It took the passage of time and the changing ways of a nation to redirect the course of Kentucky life. Indicative of this was a melancholy soliloquy by

Superintendent of Public Instruction H. A. M. Henderson in which he wrote, "A little square unhewed log building ablaze in the sun, standing upon the dusty highway or some bleak and barren spot that had been robbed of every tree and blossoming shrub, without yard, fence, or other surroundings suggestive of comfort to abate its bare, cold, hard and hateful look, is fit representative of the district schoolhouses of the Commonwealth. . . ." These were hardly fit temples for John D. Taylor's "fireflies at summer sunset," but rather were makeshift abodes against whose dingy walls flickered crude candles of learning for a people held captive by an arrested agrarian past.

7

THE CENTRAL THEME
IN MYTH AND REALITY

THE CENTRAL THEME of Kentucky history is politics. No aspect of life in the commonwealth has escaped its influence. In some areas the impact has been so subtle that historians have had to be alert to detect it. In more secular affairs the political impress has been made by bold and aggressive personalities and in the face of crisis issues. Masses of Kentuckians have revealed their reactions to politics half in deadly seriousness and half in whimsical jest. Over the span of two centuries Kentucky political personalities have ranged from dignified and mature statesmen to buffoons who campaigned for the fun of it. The state's political hustings evolved from those crude brawls associated with periodic early militia musters to alcohol-blurred barbecues and burgoos, to present-day stylized and colorless television "debates." Lusty rural voters have cheered cutting repartee that reflects the off-color legacy of rowdy country campaigns. Such talk was far more apt to catch voter attention than would scholarly analyses of pressing issues. Kentucky political meetings before 1920 were tooth and fang encounters after the style of frontier tests of marksmanship, horse racing, and fist and skull fights. The louder the noise a candidate made, the more promising he appeared to many voters.

It may be that the only certainty about Kentucky politics, aside from its persistence as a folk art, is the fact that over the long range there has been woeful lack of common policies, of clearly defined state objectives, and of leadership that looked beyond the petty problems which concerned blocks of rural voters. Kentucky farmers seldom if ever espoused a common cause as a cohesive and organized body. Those from the more prosperous counties were hardly communicative with their "pauper" county counterparts. In a highly perceptive address to a rural Chautauqua audience in western Kentucky in 1913, H. H. Cherry, president of the Western Kentucky Normal School, said "The policy for the development of Kentucky has been too indefinite, negative and vague. Our civic, social and industrial standards have been too frequently made by men who have appealed to the prejudice and ignorance of the people rather than by a consideration of the fundamentals of permanent and universal development." Cherry said Kentucky held too many elections and suffered too much politicking. Vilifying and abusive campaigns often paralyzed the state's business and destroyed both community ideals and cooperation.

Since Kentucky gained statehood there have been at least a half dozen political crises of extended importance. These have ranged from creating a commonwealth out of a wild frontier territory, to forthright legislation in mid-twentieth century to redeem the state's poor educational image, to breaking the economic and social inertia of geographical isolation by building farm-to-market roads. Behind each crisis have been three well-defined facts. The nature of the land and its agrarian occupants has exercised strong and localized influence on both constitution-making and legislation. In every decade, and in almost every major election since 1792, there have emerged strong personalities, for better or for worse, who have dominated the political process. Finally, central issues often have arisen out of the fact that both citizens and public servants failed to act in time to prevent a growing crisis from becoming seriously injurious to the general welfare. One reads the collective Acts of the Kentucky General Assembly, the compiled statute laws, and the files of Kentucky newspapers with the realization that the agrarian presence has been historically strong and decisive. It would be challenging indeed to isolate a public act of commitment which openly defied Kentucky's vested rural and agricultural interests.

No matter how much historians have written about the developing democratic process related to the rise of the New West in the national political firmament, Kentucky from the outset has been a hunting ground for seekers of political and economic power. This truth was eloquently revealed in the prestate struggle between the overlords of the Transylvania Colony and the more forceful Virginia group led by George Rogers Clark and backed by influential land speculators. Subsequently there were the actors and issues involved in separating the western territory from Virginia. Concentric power struggles were engendered by the roguish attempt to ally the West with Spain, the dominant planter-landed interests, and the seekers after office and political prestige.

In June 1792, Kentuckians of field and furrow may have been as oblivious to the contents of the new constitution as their twentieth-century descendants are to those of the old one. But in assemblies, public debate, and the first draft of the constitution, the spirit of agrarianism and its strong-willed spokesmen was dominant. In fundamental administrative areas this fact stood out in bold relief. The basis for representation was of prime concern. It was in this operational phase of state government that the common man could hope to have his most direct say. Land titles and security of property were given the support of basic laws. No matter what philosophy may have been expressed in the Declaration of Independence, property, and landed property specifically, was a matter of high priority in Kentucky.

One can hardly reconcile the fact that Kentuckians living in the demanding physical environment of the eighteenth century turned so deaf an ear to the basic needs of the new state. The verbose debaters in and out of the conventions, who prolonged the process of constitution-making, ignored immediate needs for education, internal improvements, and general public welfare. Though an unspoken principle, the negative philosophy of waiting for nature to create the propitious moment for consideration of these obligations motivated the delegates. This fact has ever clouded the Kentucky political mind. Reflective of this conservative philosophical turn were restrictive conditions placed on legislative taxing powers. In debating the question of limiting the power of the legislators to contract public debt in excess of $500,000, Charles A. Wickliffe of Nelson County told his fellow constitutional delegates in 1849 that the state should limit its needs to modest revenue collections. Wickliffe thought each major financial demand should be satisfied only after the people had voted in favor of an appropriation. The power to tax and to appropriate was in fact the vital factor in state government and public progress itself.

One of the most interesting constitutional instruments was that devised by delegates in 1792 in the Seventh Article guaranteeing the holding of slave property. This provision was as nearly ironbound as the delegates could make it. Traditionally historians have tended to view the continuing slavery debate in Kentucky largely in the context of moral and social issues, as defined originally in the arguments and writings of Presbyterian minister David Rice. None, however, has really treated adequately the fact that slaves represented a vital labor supply for farmers in the expanding central and western agricultural counties. Remarkably, the central communities advanced from fortified stations resisting fierce Indian attacks to productive areas of rich agricultural surpluses within the scope of a decade. The passage of every year after 1775 saw slavery become economically more important in the central counties.

Drafters of Kentucky's first three constitutions were either farmers living directly under the influence of the land or country lawyers who were equally dedicated to exercising tight conservative controls. No one has stated this fact more clearly than Ira Root, a Maryland-born Louisville lawyer. Speaking before his colleagues in the Third Constitutional Convention on 12 December 1849, he said, "I wish the farming interest to be fully, fairly, and ably represented. The farming interest of the state is its great interest, nor do I believe that there is the slightest danger that any interest will ever trample over it. I believe that if the whole strength of the commonwealth was now in the hands of the citizens of Louisville, and they had a majority on this floor, that the farming interest would have little or nothing to fear from their action. Since this state has been in existence, the farmers of this commonwealth have almost been entirely represented by the lawyer interest of the commonwealth, and yet I am bold and proud to affirm that the farming interest has been as well represented as though the farmers came here themselves." Down to 1890 governors' messages consisted largely of homilies on taxation and expenditures and expressions of the need for internal improvements, institutional demands, and urgent reforms—all reflecting rural public opinion.

Behind the political history of the commonwealth have lain the myths of the watchfulness of the people, the dedication of public servants, the sanctity of the ways of the land and rural life, the practice of pure democracy, and the rugged independence of grass-roots citizens. For two centuries these myths have been attacked and defended with equal passion. Among the great flutter of public letters and handbills which flowed into the office of the *Kentucky Gazette* in the early years one critic of the common man observed that some voters "are extremely stupid, if we ask them are you going to [*sic*] Election? their answer is no, not I, I do not know the use of it I don't care who they send for delegates, those kind of men (if they may be called men or freemen) if they feel anything like oppression they are the readiest of any to growl and complain, and they will talk as if all taxation is unjust." This critic also noted that when these voters did turn out for an election they were influenced by "vile designing men [who] can toll them out like hogs and for the sake of a drink of whiskey they would sell their country not knowing what they are doing." No doubt this cynic looked forward to the day when "an evil designing man" in the twentieth century would get caught with a box containing 25,000 one dollar bills with which to toll "stupid sellers of the Commonwealth" to support of his candidate. Then there were the more generous "two-dollar" tollers of the higher priced wayward sons of grass-roots democracy.

In early attempts to curb the electoral process of selecting governors and senators, there developed a fear of an "aristocracy" that sprung from the land and slavery rather than from genetics. Such a social condition had existed in Virginia, and the fertile lands of central and western Kentucky promised a much firmer base of continued agricultural production than did the thinner sandy soils of the eastern Tidewater. By the end of the first decade of the nineteenth century there were springing up from the land men of political power and influence such as John Breckinridge, Isaac Shelby, Green Clay, Benjamin Logan, Alexander S. Bullitt, James Garrard, Henry Clay, and Levi and Thomas Todd. Already these leaders had become country squires, many of whom combined farming with the practice of a profession. The two older border heroes, Isaac Shelby and Green Clay, were very practical farmers who wielded impressive political power.

From its inception the Kentucky political system was country based; the county, with its centralizing courthouse offices, became a seat of power, working both upward to the state level and downward to the rural communities. In late 1776 the Virginia General Assembly erased the Dunmore creation of Fincastle County, and created Kentucky County, not the first in the West, but the most influential. With independent statehood in 1792 nine counties were subdivided from the original. By that date there was a scattered population of 72,825, with each tiny island of settlement threatening to become a new county, thereby intensifying the trauma of subdivision from which Kentucky was to suffer mightily throughout the rest of its history.

As the stream of immigration flowed in at floodtide demands grew proportionally for the creation of new counties. It was said that new counties were created so as to bring county seats within reasonably short horseback rides of every citizen. Some slight precedent favored the arguments of county organizers. It was political isolation which had stimulated separation of the western Kentucky District from Virginia. Distance and accessibility, however, were by no means the only reasons for the creation of new counties. As each county was organized it became an enclave of rural political power through local officeholding, the functions of magisterial and county courts, polarization of local community life, and, most important of all, control over assessing and taxing processes. Political subdivision became a vainglorious fixation until the creation of McCreary County in 1912. There was another argument for counties indicated in a letter to the *Kentucky Gazette*, 28 August 1788, in which the author said, "It would be inconceivably to the advantage of a small number of men in Fayette if all Kentucky was included in one county, and obliged to assemble here 12 times a year." This implied correctly the economic significance of the monthly meetings of the county court, when farmers brought in livestock and products for sale and patronized the county seat's merchants.

In 1840 ninety counties existed, and within the next nine years ten more were created. In the Constitutional Convention of 1849 ensued an extensive discussion of the wisdom of creating so many counties. It was suggested that no county be created which contained less than 400 square miles, which would have limited the number to 100. The limit was finally reduce to 350 square miles. With much wisdom Edward L. Mayes of Graves County spoke directly to the point when he told his fellow delegates: "If the people of Kentucky have, by an experience of fifty years, which they have had under the existing constitution, learned the deficiency of that instrument, and if they have felt a necessity for the amendment in any one particular, they have unquestionably ascertained the fact that it is exceedingly defective in not having in it some such principle of restriction as the one which the committee propose to incorporate in the new one—such a feature as will, in some degree, restrain the legislature in that wild and reckless course of policy heretofore indulged in the creation of new counties—such a feature as will give peace to the state and to people of the different counties upon these vexatious, disturbing, and distracting questions of division—such a principle, sir, as will save to the state treasury, and consequently to the people, large sums of money which will otherwise be uselessly and most improvidently expended and taken from the treasury, and from the expenditure of which no earthly good will arise, either in a public or private point of view, but much very much, of evil." Mayes was a true prophet. He cited the fact that there were twenty-one "pauper" counties then taking more from the state treasury than they collected in taxes, and there were sixteen others which collectively paid in less than $5,000. At no place did the agrarian political hand rest more heavily than in sustaining what was admittedly an inefficient system of local government. It still rests there with an all but unrelenting grip.

Fundamental weaknesses in the 1792 constitution were revealed well before the trial period of five years had elapsed, when it was to be determined whether the document should be revised. The constitution proved deficient in the three basic areas of governmental operation. There was dissatisfaction with the mode of electing governors and senators, a problem which was magnified in the confused gubernatorial election of 1796. None of the four candidates for the office received a majority; Benjamin Logan, the famous pioneer, received only a slight plurality. The ensuing dispute, in which Logan was denied the office, was a jarring incident in the history of the commonwealth. Logan seemed to have been legitimately elected governor. The somewhat complex court system was entangled in a maze of overlapping and confused jurisdictions. Almost as important was the fact that penurious legislators had provided the most niggardly rate of pay, too low to attract competent public servants no matter what the hours of office. In this era of active land litigation the significance of a defective court system was brought home directly to the humblest landholder.

Any prudent Kentuckian in 1796 had to realize that constitutional revision was inescapable. Nevertheless, the powerful agrarian voice of the Bluegrass opposed revision. This influential group was not oblivious to the need, but rather it feared injury to its special interest. Slaveowners looked upon

Article Seven as their bulwark of protection. This "aristocratic" proslavery opposition was powerful, but not enough so to permit an adamant stand in opposition to a new convention call. Thus in a complete reversal of position the strong agrarian leaders of the central counties promoted a call for a new convention and mustered enough strength to mandate the changes which would be acceptable. In a new constitution additional safeguards were to be given to slavery, the sanctity of the constitution itself, and state expenditures. In keeping with the past, delegates made no provisions for public education, internal improvements, or any form of social services. The process of government was restricted to the barest essentials for maintaining the political state. The new document was in time to prove enormously important as a precedent. In the half century of its existence Kentucky functioned under institutional handicaps which became almost disastrously pronounced in the long range of its history. In these five decades, when there was little or no industrial and urban challenge to the agrarian establishment the bases of power became well established.

During the first half of the nineteenth century at least a half dozen cardinal issues troubled the Kentucky political waters. The first of these was the expansionist or antianglophile crusade led by legislator Henry Clay, who sought to bring about the establishment of a self-contained American economic system in which Kentucky farmers would be key supporters. This dramatic and no doubt demagogic move, in which he appeared in the General Assembly clad in homespun, led directly into an even more important era of American expansionism. The resulting War of 1812 brought prosperity, and subsequently disaster to Kentuckians. Overproduction of agricultural products, accrual of heavy personal debts, heedless speculation in lands, and an optimism based on misconceptions of the new national economic and industrial forces proved ruinous. Thus agrarian Kentucky by 1818 was caught in a well-nigh untenable economic position.

In public documentary collections of the commonwealth remains buried much of the complex history of the "relief-anti-relief" debacle of the decade 1817–27. Kentucky's agricultural economy was entrapped in a crushing political and banking power struggle. At no time have citizens, bankers, legislators, and merchants acted with more economic naiveté than in dealing with the great panic of 1819. Political lines became clearly drawn in this decade, and they have generally endured to date with only internal factional and partisan shiftings and regroupings. In the three decades from 1820 to 1850 the whole American social and economic system underwent enormous changes. Inventions and industrial technology began to make new approaches to national problems of expansion and economics. These decades of vast geographical expansion drained off significant numbers of Kentuckians. The application of steam power to manufacturing and transportation caught Kentucky too severely undercapitalized to take advantage of its fortunate geographic location or to begin exploiting its rich natural resources. Only Louisville and Covington in these years made modest urban expansions. Although these towns received European immigrants, agricultural Kentucky reaped little if any benefit from the newcomers. In fact, rural Kentucky nativism opposed the coming of Germans and Irish to the Ohio Valley.

In the early years of this era Americans in many parts of the nation actively concerned themselves with the development of their social institutions. In Kentucky small groups of concerned individuals sought to spur such development, but they were too few and poorly representative of the state as a whole. Even some of the governors recognized the need for progress in public education, care of dependent persons, and state management of criminals. Dorothea Lynde Dix, the famous pioneer social reformer, visited the legislature in 1845 to make an appeal for humane care of socially dependent Kentuckians, but without major influence. County jails and the penitentiary remained as medieval as ever, and so did the care of the insane and feebleminded. Politically Kentucky seemed to be caught up in a lethargy from which it neither could nor wanted to escape.

There is no dependable standard of measurement by which

to determine the loss of talent and human resources caused by outward migration before 1850, though it is easy enough to identify scores of individuals who drifted away and made tremendously important public contributions in their new homes. Part of Kentucky's loss was directly due to failure of its agrarian system to offer economic hope to ambitious youths. The historian cannot restrain himself however, from some refutation of the view that the presence of slavery in many areas of Kentucky was the only costly and stultifying long-range social and economic fact. Scarcely a traveler, native or foreign, who visited the Ohio Valley before 1860 failed to make some kind of insidious comparison between Kentucky and its free-state neighbors to the north. There are grounds, however, on which to question the basis of many of these comparisons. Not one of the states in the Old Northwest was so heavily handicapped by having so large a part of its landed area fit only for subsistence agriculture. None of them had so many seriously landlocked portions of population as Kentucky, and none was so completely off the immigration route. Finally, none was so deeply influenced by the transfer of such a fully unified older political tradition. None, with only isolated exceptions, developed in so short an interval of time a cohesive agrarian landed aristocracy which retained political leadership and held itself aloof from other elements of the state's population.

Motivated largely by fear of injury to the institution of slavery, framers of the first Kentucky Constitution included the famous Seventh Article, which made three positive guarantees. First, slavery would be assured the general protection of state law; second, anyone who chose to bring slaves into the state might do so without restrictions; third, owners and dealers could remove slaves from Kentucky at will. In 1833 the General Assembly, acting under heavy pressures to control the interstate slave trade, enacted the famous Anti-Importation Law. This law materially modified one of the above guarantees. By this date more prosperous farmers in slaveholder counties were turning more of their lands to pasturage and livestock production or to hemp production, where use of slave labor was less profitable. To the south an expanding cotton belt created an active and profitable market for Kentucky's surplus slave population and in time drew off large numbers of unneeded laborers. Finally, there was an element of social guilt about the transportation of slaves into the state for the purpose of resale in the South.

Between 1833 and 1849 the Anti-Importation Law stirred deep-seated furore among farmer slaveowners. Delegates to the Constitutional Convention of 1849 spent an inordinate amount of time discussing slavery, largely within the context of chattel property. In fact, some delegates declared the main purpose of the convention was to devise an unassailable safe-guard for the institution. When a delegate spoke to the point that the people had the power to restructure their government at any time he provoked bitter exchanges; frequently the convention went into the committee of the whole to discuss slave issues. William Chenault, a Madison County farmer, said in one of the exchanges, "If we attempt to engraft the law of 1833 upon your constitution, what does it intimate? It is, sir, that we are resolved to change the organic law, by engraving upon it a feature which, if carried out, will strike at the very root of slavery in this confederacy. Yes, sir, and this un-derstanding produces alarm. Even while we are consuming time here in debate, there is not a Kentucky slaveholder—there is not an infant in Kentucky, of ten years of age who does not feel that his rights and his property are somewhat endangered by this convention." The will of the agrarian slaveholders prevailed, for the most part in the new Article Ten. The right of slave property was positively guaranteed and reluctantly the legislature was empowered to pass an anti-importation law. Otherwise the institution of slavery remained unaltered.

Few issues in Kentucky political history have generated more emotions than that of proportioning legislative and con-gressional districts. On this ground rural and urban Kentuck-ians have contested for position since 1849. As the Ohio River tier from Covington to Louisville gained in population the agrarian leadership became apprehensive of a shift in political control of the state. When delegates came to consider apportionment on 10 November 1849, Squire Turner, a lawyer-farmer of Madison County and an ardent proslavery apostle, stirred some delegates to anger with a narrowly provincial speech. He professed belief in the principle of proportional representation, but on highly restricted terms. He said, "The southern and interior portions of the state are, and ever will be agricultural. An agricultural population is never so dense as a manufacturing and commercial one. Now take the people along the Ohio from one extreme of the state to the other, including the cities and a strip of territory ten miles in width along that line, and their pursuits will ultimately be commercial and manufacturing, and are so now to a considerable extent. What is the great and predominating interest that should be secured by our policy here? It is the agricultural—the rights of those who have invested their capital in agriculture. But unless we adopt some safeguards, the time will come when that interest will be entirely subservient to the commercial and manufacturing interests of the state." This in essence has been the prevailing attitude toward urban political influences, especially those originating in Louisville.

Squire Turner was reading the population statistics of communities along the Ohio. There was a great inflow of foreign immigrants who, in his view, were of lesser human quality than the rural Kentucky population and would prove antagonistic toward slavery. He wrongly believed that the slave population was shrinking. "Mark who are taking the place of the black population," he said, "and observe the feelings of the great portion of the people who are filling up these manufacturing towns and cities all along the river. They are generally hostile to the institution of slavery, and disposed to go hand-in-hand with its enemies who live across the river." To check the insidious influence of foreign-born immigrants Squire Turner proposed that Jefferson County and Louisville be allotted one senatorial district, or 1/38 vote in Kentucky government. Quickly the Louisville delegates charged him with proposing to discriminate against the Ohio River population, which he called servants, tavern waiters, and laborers. The population of Louisville he said was "constantly migratory—is unstable, and feels very little community of interest with native Kentuckians. It is here to-day and gone to-morrow." Its influence, he thought, should be controlled. "Shall we allow one city, if it grows large enough, to govern the whole state?" he asked of the convention. At that moment Louisville and Jefferson County had a combined population of approximately 60,000; in the past decade the number had precisely doubled. Of the total number 47,000 were white, and 15,782 had been born in Europe. Kentucky had a total white population in 1850 of 761,413. Louisville alone had a population of 43,194, compared with 12,000 in Lexington, 9,408 in Covington, and 411 in Richmond. Louisville accounted for approximately half the value of manufactured goods produced in Kentucky and paid into the state treasury nearly twice as much revenue as three other senatorial districts.

Senator John Hargis, delegate from the isolated mountain counties of Morgan and Breathitt, supported Turner by proposing all Kentucky cities be held firmly in an agrarian grip until their populations exceeded 300,000. Thus the sectional pattern for the future was shaped. The districting formula written into the new constitution was fairly complex, but it was clear that agrarian delegates did not propose to relinquish control of Kentucky's political system. Furthermore, the formula was placed almost beyond revision, and certainly the time lag in making changes gave rural districts a strong and lingering majority control.

The agrarian tradition survives in Kentucky in nostalgia and in political memory rather than in the actualities of economics and conditions of the land. World War I brought revolution in the forms of internal changes and national pressures. The new age served not an old and subsistence agrarian culture, but a rising urban-industrial society which developed a new set of social and political mores—mores which gestured to the past but served the expediencies of the moment. Predominant among the emerging power brokers were mining and manufacturing industries, horse racing, distilling, highway contractors, and social reformists, such as the antiparimutuel, Jockey Club, and prohibition crusaders. Out of these emergent interests arose bipartisan and special interest combines which allied the new age with the agrarian past to control the state at the executive, legislative, and county seat levels. The new controllers nurtured agrarian myths with fidelity when it served their purposes.

It is much easier to identify lingering agrarian influences in voter reactions to constitutional and political changes. Repeatedly the rural vote has figured heavily in defeating attempts either to rewrite or sharply to revise the outmoded agrarian constitution of the 1890s. Only by inscrutable political manipulation from the power wielders in Frankfort was Kentucky saved from disaster by the throttling salary and debt limitations of $5,000 and $500,000, respectively. On a broader front Kentucky entered its new industrial and economic age shackled to a past in which agrarian interests attempted to maintain as fully as possible a legal status quo which would hold the state in social and political thraldom. Historically this has resulted in the creation of a quasi-legal condition in which Kentucky has come to operate more and more under an extraordinary and perhaps extralegal commission form of government. Only in this way has it been possible to survive constitutional limitations without destroying the illusion of constitutionality itself. Agrarian legislative needs are now served by legislators responding to pressures of farmer groups, rather than by direct representation. In any event the legalistic demands of the new agriculture vary little in fundamentals from those of the new urban-industrial society. The whole government structure has become more or less professional, with lawyers, not farmers, largely in control of the legislative and administrative processes.

Ira Root, Louisville lawyer and constitutional delegate, was indeed prescient in 1849 when he told his colleagues, "Since this state has been in existence the farmers of this commonwealth have almost entirely been represented by the lawyer interest of the commonwealth, and yet I am bold and proud to affirm that the farming interest has been just as well represented as though the farmers came here personally themselves. It is not therefore that particular interests shall be represented, it is that men of sense, of experience, of enlightened views and of sound policy, shall be sent here, and if they all come from one corner of the state, I apprehend no man would ever prove so recreant to his own interest, as to violate any of the great principles that operate to secure the best interest of the farmer."

Legions of actors have trod the Kentucky political stage. From countless "stumps" the voices of giants and pygmies have cried out in anguish, in anger, and in accusation. Before them have stood rural multitudes listening to horrendous descriptions of the state's social and economic plight, and to promises that if elected "the men of the people" would quickly set things aright in Frankfort. The "people" have wandered down from the hills and out of the hollows, from Bluegrass meadows, across Pennyroyal swales, and from Mississippi River swamps to be assured that salvation was no further away than the next election. Like the sons of Esau and of Jacob, yeoman voters have returned home cheered by assurances they were honest, hard-laboring, God-fearing men, the pillars of Kentucky society. Kentucky yeomanry has continually cherished the prospect that rising generations of politicians would "turn the rascals out of office" and replace them with dedicated servants from the ranks of common men. Even more pleasing has been the illusion that a fresh generation of public servants would enrich Kentucky life and institutions without burdening the people with new taxes.

From that natal moment when the first backwoods orator mounted the podium in convention to argue for the creation of an independent commonwealth a notable succession of clamoring speakers has expounded the glories of the political future. Leading their constituencies in and out of crises, these masters have ever paid tribute to the basic precept that the agrarian way of life was the wholesome way. They promised never to tax it out of existence or to bring it under threat of revolutionary change. In legislative halls, the governor's office, and on the hustings the cause of agrarian Kentucky has been equated with motherhood itself.

Bibliographical Note

ALTHOUGH the bibliography of Kentucky history has grown rather extensive over the years, it is strange that no one has written a general book on agriculture. Fortunately some special studies deal with both agriculture and rural life in the commonwealth. The papers of such public men as John Brown, Isaac Shelby, John Breckinridge, and Henry Clay reflect how intimately the agricultural welfare of Kentuckians was interwoven with the politics of American western expansion.

The good manuscript collections in the Wilson Collection in the Margaret I. King Library, the collections of early governors' papers in the Kentucky Historical Society, and the manuscripts in the Filson Club are all important basic sources of information about the expansion of frontier Kentucky. After 1790 the decennial *Reports* of the United States Bureau of the Census give an ever-broadening statistical profile of the state's social and economic conditions. These I have used extensively.

Three official Kentucky publications are indispensable in the consideration of rural life in the commonwealth. These are the *Acts* and *Journals* of the General Assembly, the annual reports of the state auditor, and the post-Civil War reports of the Commissioner of Agriculture and Labor. Too, the published series of Kentucky *Documents* are rich sources describing affairs of the people. All of these, including the original tax and auditors' reports contained in the Department of Archives, I have used.

Reflective of the intellectual and cultural growth of Kentucky communities are the *Reports* of the Superintendents of

Public Instruction. Since 1870 these annual summaries consti-
tute a documentary history of Kentucky education. This is
especially true of those between 1890 and 1916.

Several early histories comprise largely contemporary views
of the state. Among these are John Filson's *History of Ken-
tucke* (1784); both editions of Humphrey Marshall's *The History of Kentucky* (1812; 2 vols., 1824); Mann Butler, *History
of the Commonwealth of Kentucky* (1834 and 1836). To a
certain extent this is true of Lewis Collins, the *History of Kentucky* (1847; 2 vols., 1874). Four local histories are rich in information about key Kentucky localities. These are H. M'mur-
tries, *Sketches of Louisville and Its Environs* (1819); Benjamin
Cassedy, *History of Louisville, from Its Earliest Settlement till
the Year 1852* (1852); William Henry Perrin, ed., *History of
Fayette County Kentucky with an Outline Sketch of the
Bluegrass Region* (1882); and Charles R. Staples, *The History
of Pioneer Lexington* (1939).

There is a rather large volume of sources relating to the
economic and diplomatic struggle to open the Mississippi
River to free use by American farmer-boatmen. The best of
these are James Wilkinson, *Memoirs of My Own Times* (1816);
William Littell, *Political Transactions in and Concerning Kentucky* (1806); J. M. Brown, *Political Beginnings of Kentucky*
(1889); Patricia Watlington, *The Partisan Spirit, Kentucky
Politics, 1779–1792* (1972); John D. Barnhart, *Valley of Democracy, the Frontier versus the Plantation in the Ohio Valley, 1775–1818* (1953); Lowell Harrison, *John Breckinridge,
Jeffersonian Republican* (1969); Dumas Malone, *Jefferson the
President, First Term, 1801–1805* (1970); and by far the most
revealing, Arthur P. Whitaker, *The Mississippi Question,
1795–1803*. Erik F. Haites, James Mak, and Gary M. Walton,
*Western River Navigation: The Era of Early Internal De-
velopment 1810–1860* (1976) is a most useful economic analysis
of early use of the Ohio and Mississippi rivers.

Kentucky from the outset attracted both domestic and
foreign travelers. Among the travel accounts used in this text
are Gilbert Imlay, *A Topographical Description of the West-

ern Country of North America (1792); Francois Andre Michaux, *Travels to the West of the Alleghany Mountains in the States of Ohio, Kentucky, and Tennessee* (1804); Jedediah Morse, *The American Geography; or, a View of the United States of America* (1792); Harry Toulmin, *The Western Country in 1793; Reports of Kentucky and Virginia* (1794), *A Description of Kentucky in North America* (1792); Fortesque Cuming, *Sketches of a Tour to the Western Country, through the States of Ohio and Kentucky* (1810); Henry Bradshaw Fearon, *Sketches of America* (1818); and Timothy Flint, *Recollections [sic] of the Last Ten Years* (1826).

Although there is no general history of Kentucky agriculture and industry, there are some significant monographs. Among them are James F. Hopkins, *A History of the Hemp Industry in Kentucky* (1951); William Axton, *Tobacco and Kentucky* (1975); Joseph Clark Robert, *The Story of Tobacco in America* (1949). The history of the livestock industry in the state, like that of agriculture, has not received as much attention as it deserves. Two farm journals, *The Franklin Farmer*, 1839–1842, and the *Western Farmer*, 1840–1845, are basic sources of information for the years when Kentuckians were excited over livestock breeding. Important books are Alvin F. Sanders, *Short-Horn Cattle, a Series of Historical Sketches, Memoirs, and Records of the Breed and Its Development in the United States and Canada* (1901); Anna Virginia Parker, *The Sanders Family of Grass Hills* (1966); William Warfield, *American Shorthorn Importations Containing the Pedigrees of all Short Horn Cattle Hitherto Imported to America* (1884). An amazingly fine scholarly discussion of the American livestock industry, with emphasis on Kentucky, is James Westfall Thompson's "A History of Livestock Raising in the United States, 1607–1860," *Agricultural History Series*, no. 5, 1942, vols. 1–7 (1942). The famous University of Chicago medievalist demonstrated a facility for writing in another field. A book of broad sectional nature, but rich in Kentucky materials, is Lewis C. Gray, *History of Agriculture in the Southern States*, 2 vols. (1932). A vivid sense of the woes of some Ken-

133

tucky farmers is contained in John G. Miller, *The Black Patch War* (1936); and James O. Nall, *The Tobacco Night Riders of Kentucky and Tennessee, 1905–1909* (1940).

The personal story of Kentucky has been more fully developed than any other aspect of state history. Most pertinent to this study are Charles Talbert, *Benjamin Logan, Kentucky Frontiersman* (1962); John Bakeless, *Daniel Boone, Master of the Wilderness* (1939); William C. Davis, *Breckinridge: Statesman, Soldier, Symbol* (1974); James F. Hopkins and Mary Wilma Hargreaves, eds., *The Papers of Henry Clay* 5 vols. (1959–1973); Cassius M. Clay, Jr., *The Addresses and Writings of Cassius M. Clay, Jr.* (1914); Grant C. Knight, *James Lane Allen and the Genteel Tradition* (1940); James A. Ramage, *John Wesley Hunt, Pioneer Merchant, Manufacturer and Financier* (1974); Frances L. Dugan and Jacqueline Bull, *Bluegrass Craftsman, being the Reminiscences of Hiram Stedman* (1959); Shelby S. Elam, *Kentucky thru Thick and Thin* (1955); and Urey Woodson, *The First New Dealer: William Goebel, His Origin, Ambitions, Achievements, His Assassination . . .* (1939).

There is a considerable volume of religious history pertaining to Kentucky. The more significant works are John B. Boles, *The Great Revival, 1787–1805* (1972); Catharine C. Cleveland, *The Great Revival in the West, 1797–1805* (1916); W. E. Arnold, *A History of Methodism in Kentucky*, 3 vols. (1935); John Taylor, *A History of Ten Baptist Churches, of Which the Author Has Been Alternately a Member* (1823); M. J. Spalding, *Sketches of the Early Catholic Missions in Kentucky* (1844); and Lucian V. Rule, *An Old Country Church, Its Traditions and Ideals* (1915).

There is a sizable library of materials relating to the history of education in Kentucky. Important basic early sources are the *Report of the Debates and Proceedings of the Convention for the Revision of the Constitution of the State of Kentucky 1849,* (1849); *The Reports and Proceedings in the Kentucky Constitutional Convention*, 4 vols. (1891); *Acts*, Kentucky General Assembly, 1821–1970; Barksdale Hamlet, *History of Education in Kentucky* (1914); Frank L. McVey,

The Gates Open Slowly (1949); C. W. Hackensmith, *Out of Time and Tide, the Evolution of Education in Kentucky* (1970), *Public Education in Kentucky* (1922); Jesse Stuart, *The Thread That Runs So True* (1974); *Report of the Kentucky Educational Commission* (1933); and William F. DeMoss, "Wiping Out Illiteracy in Kentucky," *The Illustrated World*, vol. 24 (1916). The clearest concept of year-to-year educational history is contained in the *Reports of the State Superintendent of Public Instruction* (1870–1976).

The quality of family life in Kentucky as related to rural areas is measured in several primary and secondary sources. The most important, of course, are the decennial *Reports* of the United States Census Bureau and the annual *Statistical Abstracts of the United States*. I relied heavily on these sources. Special studies are M. Bauder Ward, *Characteristics of Families on Small Farms* (1956); Robert E. Galloway, *Part-Time Farming in Eastern Kentucky* (1956); Irvin T. Sanders and Robert E. Galloway, *Rural Families in the Purchase Area of Western Kentucky* (1956); Mary B. Willeford, *Income and Health in Remote Rural Areas* (1932). In a broader vein H. H. Cherry touched on the quality of Kentucky country life in his address *A Greater Kentucky* (1913); and John L. Johnson presented it in a fuller economic context in *Income in Kentucky Counties: Distribution by Amount, by Type, and by Size* (1955). Good historical perspective on origins are John D. Barnhart, "Frontiersmen and Planters in the Foundation of Kentucky," *Journal of Southern History* 7 (February 1941): 19–36; and Henry P. Scalf, *Kentucky's Last Frontier* (1966).

Politics has touched Kentucky rural life as much as any other aspect of the commonwealth's history. There is a considerable body of material on this subject, but more immediately reflective are Robert Ireland, *The County Courts in Antebellum Kentucky* (1972) and *The County in Kentucky History* (1976); R. E. Hughes, F. W. Schaefer, and E. L. Williams, *That Kentucky Campaign; or the Law, the Ballot and the People in the Goebel-Taylor Contest* (1900); Jasper B. Shannon and Ruth McQuown, *Presidential Politics in Kentucky, 1824–1948* (1950); Nollie Olin Taft, *History of State*

Revenue and Taxation in Kentucky (1931). A broad spectrum of Kentucky agrarian politics exists in *Official Report of the Proceedings and Debates in the Convention Assembled in Frankfort, on the Eighth Day of September, 1890, to Adopt, Amend or Change the Constitution of Kentucky*, 4 vols. (1891). The *Acts*, Kentucky General Assembly, 1792–1976, are indispensable sources of information for the legal aspects of the history of agrarian Kentucky, and these I have consulted frequently and generously.

The literary history of Kentucky has been treated in various forms. John Wilson Townsend, *Kentucky in American Letters, 1784–1975*, compiled and edited by Dorothy Edwards Townsend, 3 vols. (1976), is a good bibliographical listing of Kentucky writers. The novels and other works by various authors referred to in the text are readily available in libraries throughout the state. Mary Verhoff in *The Kentucky Mountains* (1911) and *The Kentucky River Navigation* (1917) gave a searching report on the social and economic facts of the region. In an older socio-historical manner, J. W. Haney, *The Mountain People of Kentucky* (1906), tried to account for folk origins and adaptations to the land.